"Understand Revelation In One Day"

Roger Miller, M.D.

Derek Press

Printed by Derek Press, Cleveland Tennessee

ISBN: 1-59684-096-X

Printed by Derek Press, Cleveland, TN

Printed in the United States of America

Contents

Chapters

Preface

This book is not a substitute for reading the Book of
Revelation as it is written in the Holy Bible. Although most of
Revelations verses from the New King James version of the Bible
are given, some were summarized and reviewed in narrative form.
The Book of Revelation and its particular wording is so important
that a stern warning is given to those who make copies from the
original scroll.

**"If anyone adds to these things, God will add to him the
plagues that are written in this book; and if anyone takes
away from the words of the book of this prophecy, God shall
take away his part from the Book of Life, from the holy city,
and from the things which are written in this book"
(Revelation 22:18-19).**

Understanding Revelation in One Day is only intended to be a
study aid that can be read by the average reader in three to four
hours. I would recommend that this be done by reading chapters
one and two in the evening (1 hour) followed by chapters three
and four the next morning (1 hour). At noon time read chapter
five (30 minutes) and finish the book before sundown by reading
chapters six and seven (1 hour). Within one day (a Biblical day is
from sunset to sunset) you will discover the message of
Revelation and its relevance for your life. Are you ready?

Acknowledgments

I would like to thank all the people that made this book possible. First to my wife and best friend, Valerie, whose loving support was vital to this project, also to my children Chasity, Michelle, Roger, Paul and especially Kelly who helped edit and proof the manuscript (and who appears on the cover as the symbolic woman of the faithful church). And, finally, to my father and mother, Paul and Myrna, who raised me to love Jesus.

Chapter 1

Introduction and Greetings from Heaven
Revelation Chapter 1:1-8

"And war broke out in heaven: Michael and his angels fought against the dragon; and the dragon and his angels fought, but they did not prevail, nor was a place found for them in heaven any longer. So the great dragon was cast out, that serpent of old, called the Devil and Satan, who deceives the whole world; he was cast to the earth, and his angels were cast out with him…Therefore rejoice, O heavens, and you who dwell in them! Woe to the inhabitants of the earth and the sea! For the devil has come down to you, having great wrath, because he knows that he has a short time" (Revelation 12:7- 9, 12).

Understanding Revelation in one day–Wow! Is that possible? With its signs and symbols, strange images of beasts, scenes of heaven and judgments upon the earth, is it possible to make any sense out of all this? I believe it is not only possible, but guaranteed. Here is why. God wants us to know its meaning!

Although the book of Revelation was written nearly two thousand years ago, its message is most urgent for us today. Right now God wants the last generations living on the earth to hear and understand these important words of prophecy. Through the reading and study of this book you will discover its secrets and open a new door of understanding and faith you never thought possible!

Let's read the first verse:

"The Revelation of Jesus Christ, which God gave Him to show His servants—things which must shortly take place" (Revelation 1:1).

As you can see, Revelation is a message about our future that God wants us to know. In fact, the word, *'Revelation'* itself means, *'to unveil, to uncover,* and *to make known'*. However,

Revelation's inspired prophecies are from a spiritual God and it is only God who can help us understand them! As we gain knowledge of His word and allow His Spirit to reveal its truth, what was once a mystery will become clear. But this is conditional; only those who sincerely seek truth with a willing heart will find it. Before we go any further in our study, let's read a few scriptures to help establish these important points regarding Revelation's inspired origin, its spiritual nature and the requirements for understanding its truths.

Through inspiration, God gives prophecy for the purpose of being understood and having value to those who read it. In 2 Timothy 3:16, 17 we read this

"All Scripture is given by inspiration of God, and is profitable for doctrine, for reproof, for correction, for instruction in righteousness, that the man of God may be complete, thoroughly equipped for every good work."

Both the Old and New Testament were given by inspiration from God. Not two different Gods but the same God, the God of creation. Through all of scripture we will find His truth for mankind.

"God, who at various times and in different ways spoke in time past to the fathers by the prophets, has in these last days spoken to us by His Son, whom He has appointed heir of all things, through whom also He made the worlds" (Hebrews 1:1-2).

And finally in 2 Peter:

"We also have the prophetic word made more sure, which you do well to heed as a light that shines in a dark place, until the day dawns and the morning star rises in your hearts; knowing this first, that no prophecy of Scripture is of any private interpretation, for prophecy never came by the will of man, but holy men of God spoke as they were moved by the Holy Spirit" (2 Peter 1:19-21)

As you can see, we cannot on our own know the will of God;

it must come from God Himself through His prophets. For over a thousand years, from the writing of Genesis to the book of Revelation, God has inspired men with His thoughts, which they recorded as the Holy Scripture. Through dreams and visions, holy men of God spoke as His Spirit moved them. Scripture is from a Spiritual God and its spiritual message can only be understood as the Spirit of God reveals its truth to our mind. No matter how 'smart' we are or what our IQ is, without the Spirit of God we will never 'figure it out'.

"These things we also speak, not in words which man's wisdom teaches but which the Holy Spirit teaches, comparing spiritual things with spiritual. But the natural man does not receive the things of the Spirit of God, for they are foolishness to him; nor can he know them, because they are spiritually discerned" (1 Corinthians 2:13-14).

Of course, we still have to study God's word carefully and diligently. We need to know what it says and be able to compare scripture with scripture in our quest for truth. Also this will help us separate in our thinking what is truly a part of Holy Scripture and what are merely the opinions and teachings of men.

"Be diligent to present yourself approved to God, a worker who does not need to be ashamed, rightly dividing the word of truth. But shun profane and vain babblings, for they will increase to more ungodliness. And their message will spread like cancer" (2 Timothy 2:15-17).

It is important to "rightly divide" scripture. In other words, find it's true meaning by studying the context and comparing with other scriptures for a complete understanding. This certainly takes effort. Truth is like a buried treasure, we have to dig for it. This effort cannot be half hearted and must come from one who is willing to do God's will. This kind of sincerity is spoken of in Deuteronomy, Jeremiah, and John.

"But from there you will seek the Lord your God, and you will

find Him if you seek Him with all your heart and with all your soul" (Deuteronomy 4:29).

"And you will seek Me and find Me, when you search for Me with all your heart" (Jeremiah 29:13).

"If anyone wants to do His will, he shall know concerning the doctrine, whether it is from God or whether I speak on My own authority" (John 7:17).

To put it simply; if we want to obey God, we will find His truth. If you are willing to study Scripture and ask God to help you understand it, and when it is your heart's desire to know and to do His will; then God will be faithful to teach you the profound truths in the book of Revelation- today! Let's ask Him to do that right now,

Heavenly Father, we desire to know Your truth and to follow Your will. Teach us right now as we study your word and give us strength by Your Spirit to live for You – In Jesus' name–Amen.

Before we begin our study into the book of Revelation, I would like to give you five keys for successful study of Bible prophecy. These have been used for centuries to help unlock the seemingly closed doors to the interpretation of the signs and symbols often found in Revelation's prophetic imagery. These five amazing and yet simple keys will open before you new and greater levels of understanding.

Here we go, let's look at the first key.

1. When studying the prophecies of Revelation we need to realize that its signs, symbols, and stories may not be unique. They have often been borrowed from other parts of scripture and prophecy, frequently from the Old Testament. Upon close examination of the original text containing these seemingly mysterious elements, we can often find clues to understand their meaning.

This key turns out to be very helpful throughout the book

of Revelation. In fact, over half of the 404 verses in the book contain elements taken directly from Old Testament stories and prophecies.

As we study together, I will refer to these Old Testament scriptures to help you understand the book of Revelation. One example of this key's importance is related to Revelation's frequent reference to the sanctuary or temple of God in heaven. In fact, over one quarter of the verses in Revelation make some reference to this sanctuary.

As you will see, the study and understanding of the sanctuary described by Moses in the book of Exodus, will help us a great deal in understanding Revelation's meaning when referring to the heavenly sanctuary. This makes perfect sense when we read in Exodus 25:9, that it was God who gave Moses the pattern or blueprints for the sanctuary, and according to Hebrews 8:5, this 'earthly sanctuary' was to be a copy and shadow of the heavenly one.

Whenever the Bible gives the meaning of a symbol used in prophecy, this same explanation can be used in Revelation. For instance, in chapter seven of Daniel, when the angel Gabriel explains that the animal-like beasts in the prophecy were symbols used to represent kingdoms, we can also understand them to have the same meaning in the prophecies of Revelation. In fact, the whole book of Daniel with its stories and prophetic symbols will be very important to the interpretation of Revelation's prophecies.

Even within the book of Revelation itself, a symbol may be used, and later it will be explained. We need to be diligent to find these stories and their clues wherever they are found in scripture.

2. The Bible and the Bible alone can be used to interpret prophecy. We must never bring in outside sources or events and then try to fit prophecy to them. God is the

author of prophecy and has given in the Holy Scripture all
that is necessary for their understanding. We do not need
and should not use non-prophetic writings to interpret the
Bible. The third key refers to the application of Bible
prophecy.

3. Bible prophecy usually has as its primary application, the
   people and time to which it was first given. In addition,
   there is often a secondary application to the church in the
   future. Finally, there is a personal and spiritual application
   to individuals who may read the prophecy at any time in
   history. This is often used with prophecies given to the
   Jewish nation of the Old Testament. Not only did the
   prophecy apply to their time and place, but also to the
   future New Testament Church (the spiritual nation of spiritual Jews).

   In addition, the reader can receive a spiritual lesson from
   these prophecies concerning their own personal relationship with God. We will see this key used several times
   throughout the book of Revelation. Another key is the
   'repeat and expand' format found in some books of Old
   Testament prophecies.

4. This is basically the idea of repeating a prophecy for
   emphasis and then focusing on its new and expanded
   details. The repetition helps the reader organize the information of the prophecy in his/her mind. This repeat and
   expand arrangement occurs throughout the prophecies
   found in the book of Daniel. For instance, chapter two of
   Daniel gives a prophecy pertaining to the order of succes-
   sive kingdoms that would arise upon the earth. Chapter
   seven repeats this order with added detail especially relat-
   ing to the latter kingdoms. Chapter eight of Daniel again
   repeats several of these kingdoms, this time with new
   information about specific aspects of one of the kingdoms.
   Chapters nine, eleven and twelve further expand the

detailed time lines and information concerning these kingdoms. This method of teaching is very helpful for grasping deep and complex prophecies. We will see this repeat and expand method used throughout the book of Revelation as well. The fifth and final key may be the most important of all.

5. In our study of the book of Revelation we must never draw a conclusion that contradicts clear teaching of scripture elsewhere. It would be better to not understand the prophecy, than to come to a wrong understanding that is in opposition to other parts of God's Word. We must compare scripture with scripture and our conclusions must be unifying not contradictory.

Let's review. In our study of Revelation, we must be sure that we ask God to help us understand these prophetic words. In our own hearts, we must desire to know His truth and be willing to follow it. In addition, we need to study using the keys to Bible prophecy interpretation. These include finding relevant scriptures to help us understand the signs and symbols found in Revelation- we need to let the Bible interpret itself. Also, that prophecy not only applies to the time, place and people to which it was given, but also to the future church as well as having a personal application and significance. And finally, any conclusion we draw from our study of prophecy must be in harmony to the plain teaching of scripture found elsewhere. The Bible does not contradict itself. God does not change. He is the same yesterday, today and tomorrow. In Him is no shadow of turning. It is only man's various interpretations that contradict.

Ok, now we are ready to understand Revelation in one day. Let's begin.

Revelation Chapter 1

"The Revelation of Jesus Christ, which God gave Him to show His servants—-things which must shortly take place. And He sent and signified it by His angel to His servant John, who bore witness to the word of God, and to the testimony of Jesus Christ, and to all things that he saw" (Revelation 1:1-2).

There are three points that need to be made from these two verses.

The word '*Revelation*' is from the original Greek word '*apocalypse*', and as we have already stated means to '*unveil or uncover*'. This uncovering refers to Jesus Himself as well as to future events. Thus, it can be said that through the book of Revelation, we will now see or understand what has been previously hidden concerning Jesus and the future of the church.

The word '*signified*' means '*to show by a sign or symbol*'. Here we see that prophecy in Revelation will be explained using signs and symbols, which, by using the keys we have discussed, we will be able to correctly interpret.

Notice the flow of information in the verses: from God to Jesus, and then by His angel to John, and finally from John to us. Revelation is a message to us from God Himself. He would not give us an important message and not help us to understand it. In fact, the next verse pronounces a blessing on those who read and understand.

"Blessed is he who reads and those who hear the words of this prophecy, and keep those things which are written in it; for the time is near" (Revelation 1:3).

It is God's desire that we read the book of Revelation, and then, by study of scripture and insight from His Spirit, be able to hear or have understanding. You will note that it does not stop here; happiness comes from keeping or doing what we find to be true.

Notice the sense of urgency in the text by stating that the time is near. The prophecies of Revelation were soon to unfold and they were to be understood. These prophecies would extend to the last day church, to which they would have special relevance. Revelation is ultimately a last day message to a last day church and has special application to us in the 21st century. As we see the prophecies of Revelation that have come to pass (with our now nearly two thousand year perspective), our faith and belief in God's sovereignty over earth's remaining future will grow. As Jesus once said:

"Now I tell you before it comes, that when it does come to pass, you may believe that I am He" (John 13:19).

It is God's desire that we look back in history and see how He has lead in the past and how prophecy has been fulfilled. If we do this, we will have confidence to trust Him with our future in these last days.

"John, to the seven churches which are in Asia: Grace to you and peace from Him who is and who was and who is to come, and from the seven Spirits who are before His throne, and from Jesus Christ, the faithful witness, the firstborn from the dead, and the ruler over the kings of the earth. To Him who loved us and washed us from our sins in His own blood, and has made us kings and priests to His God and Father, to Him be glory and dominion forever and ever. Amen. Behold, He is coming with clouds, and every eye will see Him, and they also who pierced Him. And all the tribes of the earth will mourn because of Him. Even so, Amen. 'I am the Alpha and the Omega, the Beginning and the End,' says the Lord, 'who is and who was and who is to come, the Almighty'" (Revelation 1:4-8).

Verses four through eight are John's greetings to the seven churches. Only ancient ruins today, these were actual Christian churches at the time Revelation was written. John wrote this book, or letter of Revelation, to the seven churches around 90 A.D. while he was a prisoner of Rome and in exile on the island of Patmos. These seven churches were located in Asia, which is now southern Turkey. Chapters two and three of Revelation, are small letters or epistles from Christ to these seven churches. We will examine these in the next chapter.

John's greeting is also a greeting from the Holy trinity in heaven: God the Father, "Him who is and who was and who is to come," God the Spirit, "the seven Spirits who are before His throne," and from God the Son, Jesus Christ, "the faithful witness, the firstborn from the dead, and the ruler over the kings of the earth." Being the true author of Revelation, God desires grace and peace to come to the church through the message of this book. Although at times the scenes and images of Revelation may be frightening, God's people are not to fear because He will be with them and supply grace that they need and a peace within their hearts.

Here also we see the first reference to God's throne room or the heavenly sanctuary:

"...the seven Spirits who are before His throne"(Revelation 1:4).

As we have already mentioned, this will be a very common scene throughout Revelation.

Let's now begin to explore this symbolism.

In the sanctuary on earth there was a seven-branched lamp stand that would provide light in its first room, the 'holy place'. This lamp stand is described in detail in Exodus 25:31-39. After its description, we read:

"And see to it that you make them according to the pattern which was shown you on the mountain"(Exodus 25:40)

The sanctuary on earth and the items associated with it were built according to the pattern shown to Moses by God. This sanctuary was to be a representation of the one in heaven, and thus illustrate God's work on man's behalf. In other words, the sanctuary and its services were a type of prophetic drama. When played out, they would figuratively demonstrate what God would do to provide salvation for fallen man. The events illustrated by the services performed in the sanctuary's courtyard would be fulfilled by Christ here on the earth. The services in the sanctuary building itself depicted those works He would do in heaven after His resurrection.

Probably the best-known symbol of the courtyard service was the lamb sacrifice. From the very beginning of scripture, God had given the innocent sacrificial lamb to be a symbol of Jesus. It was a visual lesson concerning His sacrifice and how it would make possible our forgiveness and redemption from sin. Jesus was blameless, yet He would suffer and die, receiving the wages of sin that we had earned. This act of substitution, in addition to fulfilling the justice of God's law, showed us the magnitude of God's love.

"For God so loved the world that He gave His only begotten Son..." (John 3:16).

John the Baptist, recognizing that Jesus was the fulfillment of the sacrificial lamb said this:

"Behold! The Lamb of God who takes away the sin of the world!" (John 1:29)

Not only was Jesus the Lamb at His sacrificial death on the cross, but also He would become our High Priest of the heavenly sanctuary.

"...We have such a High Priest, who is seated at the right hand of the throne of the Majesty in the heavens, a Minister of the sanctuary and of the true tabernacle which the Lord erected, and not man... [which was] the copy and shadow of the heavenly things, as Moses was divinely instructed..." (Hebrews 8:1-5).

We will have much more to say about this in later chapters, but for now let's go back to Revelation chapter one. Here in verse four we see that the Holy Spirit is the heavenly counterpart of the flame upon the seven-branched lamp stand. The Holy Spirit, which brings understanding and conviction, is appropriately symbolized as light and fire. We see this again in Revelation 4 as it describes in more detail the heavenly throne room:

"And from the throne proceeded lightnings, thunderings, and voices. And there were seven lamps of fire burning before the throne, which are the seven Spirits of God" (Revelation 4:5).

The rest of John's greeting sings praises to Jesus and makes a list of His attributes, and works on behalf of the human race.

- He is the, "faithful witness,"
- the, "firstborn from the dead,"
- the, "ruler over the kings of the earth,"
- and it is He, "who loved us and washed us from our sins in His own blood."
- He, "Has made us kings and priest to God,"
- and, "He is coming with clouds to save us,"
- He is, "The Alpha and the Omega, the beginning and the end. The one who is, and who was, and who is to come."

This list begins a theme, which will grow and expand in Revelation. Revelation will go behind the scenes to uncover God's greatest gift to man, Jesus. Throughout the book we will learn more and more about Jesus and His work in heaven on behalf of mankind.

"In My Father's house are many mansions, if it were not so, I would have told you. I go to prepare a place for you. And if I go and prepare a place for you, I will come again and receive you to Myself; that where I am, there you may be also" (John 14:2-3).

12

These well known words of Jesus, telling us that He had a work to do in heaven before He would come again to this earth, are the very theme of Revelation.

We see Jesus in Revelation as our Priest and as the High Priest in Heaven, there to intercede on our behalf and represent the faithful in the judgment. We see Him as worthy to receive authority over the kings of the earth at a heavenly inauguration and coronation. We hear his words of warning and of coming judgments to the inhabitants of the earth. And we see Him coming back to earth in great power as King of Kings.

Jesus' spectacular return to earth is the climax of Revelation's introduction. This event has been foretold throughout Holy Scripture. The following verses speak of His second coming to earth.

"For as the lightning comes from the east and flashes to the west, so also will the coming of the Son of Man be...Then the sign of the Son of Man will appear in heaven, and then all the tribes of the earth will mourn, and they will see the Son of Man coming on the clouds of heaven with power and great glory. And He will send His angels with a great sound of a trumpet, and they will gather together His elect from the four winds, from one end of heaven to the other" (Matthew 24:27, 30-31).

Paul puts it like this:

"For the Lord Himself will descend from heaven with a shout, with the voice of an archangel, and with the trumpet of God. And the dead in Christ will rise first. Then we who are alive and remain shall be caught up together with them in the clouds to meet the Lord in the air. And thus we shall always be with the Lord" (1 Thessalonians 4:16-17)

Here in Revelation, the promise that swells the heart of every believer is heard again:

"Behold, He is coming with clouds, and every eye will see Him..." (Revelation 1:7).

Jesus—the faithful witness who tells us what we need to hear and know,

Jesus—the firstborn from the dead as a guarantee to the faithful of every age that they too will come forth in the resurrection,

Jesus—the one who has regained ruler ship of the earth and gave Himself for us so that we could be made kings and priest with Him in an earth made new.

Yes! **Jesus** is coming again. And He wants you to live and reign with Him forever!

Do you desire this and would you be willing to follow Him? Through the Book of Revelation we will discover together the message and last call from Jesus to be with Him.

Chapter 2

The Seven Churches

Revelation Chapter 1: 10 through Chapter 3

"I was in the Spirit on the Lord's Day, and I heard behind me a loud voice, as of a trumpet" (Revelation 1:10).

John, in exile because of his faith, is still loyal to God. Even through tribulation John had not lost his devotion. In a spirit and attitude of worship on the Sabbath day, John receives this Revelation from heaven. Before we continue, let's take a moment and examine this topic of the Sabbath. As you will see, it will become very important later in our study of Revelation.

When on earth, Jesus had declared Himself Lord of the seventh-day Sabbath:

"For the Son of Man is Lord of the Sabbath"(Matthew 12:8–NU and M-text).

The Sabbath is the Lord's Day. Nowhere in any part of Scripture is any other day given this title. It was the seventh-day of creation that God had blessed and made holy.

"Then God blessed the seventh day and sanctified it [set apart for holy use], because in it He rested from all His work which God had created and made" (Genesis 2:3).

In the fourth commandment, which God wrote on tablets of stone, it was the Sabbath that He asked us to remember and keep holy as the Lord's day.

"Remember the Sabbath day, to keep it holy. Six days you shall labor and do all your work, but the seventh day is the Sabbath of the Lord your God…For in six days the Lord made the heavens and the earth, the sea, and all that is in them, and rested the seventh day. Therefore the Lord blessed the Sabbath day and hallowed it" (Exodus 20:8-10).

Jesus and the disciples kept the Sabbath, and after His death and resurrection it continued as a memorial of creation and part of the Christian faith.

"...the Gentiles begged that these words might be preached to them the next Sabbath...And the next Sabbath almost the whole city came together to hear the word of God" (Acts 13:42-44).

"And on the Sabbath day we went out of the city to the riverside, where prayer was customarily made; and we sat down and spoke to the women who met there" (Acts 16:13).

"And he reasoned in the synagogue every Sabbath, and persuaded both Jews and Greeks" (Acts 18:4).

The seventh-day is still the Sabbath of the fourth commandment, and as a weekly memorial of creation it calls us to remember God's authority as our creator. As promised, there remains, even today, a Sabbath rest for the people of God:

"For He has spoken in a certain place of the seventh day in this way: "And God rested on the seventh day from all His works"...There remains therefore a rest for the people of God. For he who has entered His rest has himself also ceased from his works as God did from His" (Hebrews 4:4, 9-10).

The Sabbath is a sign between God and His people. They are to remember that it is He and only He who can make them holy.

"Moreover I also gave them My Sabbaths, to be a sign between them and Me, that they might know that I am the Lord who sanctifies them... 'hallow My Sabbaths, and they will be a sign between Me and you, that you may know that I am the Lord your God" (Ezekiel 20:12,20).

In fact, observing the Sabbath becomes our acknowledgment that righteousness is by faith in the creator. Just as God is the creator of the physical world, He is also the re-creator of the spiritual. He is the only one who is able to create within us a clean and new heart. Hear the cry of David.

"Create in me a clean heart, O God, and renew a steadfast spirit within me" (Psalm 51:10).

And listen to Paul in Philippians.

"...being confident of this very thing, that He who has begun a good work in you will complete it until the day of Jesus Christ" (Philippians 1:6).

Peter has this to say:

"Therefore let those who suffer according to the will of God commit their souls to Him in doing good, as to a faithful Creator" (1 Peter 4:19).

The Sabbath teaches us to rest in God's ability as a creator. It is not by our works that we are saved, but by His.

We must be careful to not mistake the yearly Sabbaths of the ceremonial law (the seven festival Sabbaths of the old covenant, given only to the Jewish nation and spoken of in Colossians 2:16) or the fasting days (spoken of in Romans 14:5-6), with the eternal Holy Sabbath of the creation week and of the fourth commandment. The weekly Sabbath was established thousands of years before there was a Jewish nation or a Christian church. It was established at creation by God and given as a gift to all mankind. Jesus said:

"The Sabbath was made for man, and not man for the Sabbath" (Mark 2:27).

In other words, The Sabbath day was created for mankind as a gift of rest. God is the inventor of the weekend!!

Even in the earth made new, we will continue to remember the Sabbath day. The prophet Isaiah speaking of the new heavens and the new earth, (later discussed in Revelation chapter 21) says this:

"...And from one Sabbath to another, all flesh shall come to worship before Me," says the Lord" (Isaiah 66:23).

The Sabbath and true worship, by joyful obedience to God

and His law, will become very important later in our study. We will come back to this topic in more detail as it relates to Revelation's prophecies in chapter 13, but for now, let's get back to Revelation chapter one.

It is on the Sabbath day that John receives this vision from heaven, which opens before him the heavenly messenger and the message to the seven churches.

"I am the Alpha and the Omega, the First and the Last," and, "What you see, write in a book and send it to the seven churches which are in Asia" (Revelation 1:11).

As John turns to see where the voice is coming from, he sees a vision of Christ in the heavenly sanctuary. There he sees Jesus standing in the midst of the seven lampstands, which are symbolic for the seven churches:

"...the seven lampstands which you saw are the seven churches" (Revelation 1:20).

The lamps of fire burning upon the stands represent the Holy Spirit. This was described from the previous chapter as the seven spirits of fire that were before the throne of God. The Church on earth is to be filled with the symbolic oil of the Holy Spirit, and through His presence, be ignited into a flame of light and truth. It is to be a light in a dark world. Jesus is seen standing among the lampstands. This signifies to us His intense interest in His church upon the earth. Jesus has promised that He will never leave nor forsake His people. In His right hand are seen seven stars which, also according to verse 20, represent the angels of the seven churches:

"The seven stars are the angels of the seven churches"

The word, '*angel*' means, '*messenger*'. Both heavenly messengers and messengers upon the earth are assigned to deliver God's message to His people. The angels, or messengers of the churches, represent the church leaders to whom the seven letters

Roger Miller, M.D.

would be addressed. It is the strength, or right hand of Christ, which upholds the leadership of the church. Only through a submission of leadership to Christ will the works of the church be the works of Christ. However, His words (the things He will say to the churches) will be like a sharp two-edged sword. They will penetrate deep to the heart of the church's condition. Not always will these words be pleasant ones, but as a faithful and true witness Jesus must tell the church what it needs to hear. Notice that each epistle concludes that only by the Holy Spirit will the true message be received into the heart:

"He who has an ear, let him hear what the Spirit says to the churches" (Revelation 2:7).

Although each message was to a specific church, they also have future prophetic application. In other words, the churches were also symbols that represent stages the Christian church would go through before Christ would return. In addition, each message has a personal application. There will be a message to each of us, individually, for today. Will we hear what the Spirit has to say to us? Let's ask Jesus to help us hear what we need to hear today.

"Father in Heaven, open our ears to Your Spirit today. Let us hear your truth in our hearts, and give us grace to do your will. In Jesus name, Amen."

Revelation Chapter 2

The Seven Churches – The Church at Ephesus

"I know your works, your labor, your patience, and that you cannot bear those who are evil. And you have tested those who say they are apostles and are not, and have found them liars; and you have persevered and have patience, and have labored

**for My name's sake and have not become weary. Nevertheless
I have this against you, that you have left your first love.
Remember therefore from where you have fallen; repent and
do the first works or else I will come to you quickly and
remove your lampstand from its place- unless you repent. But
this you have, that you hate the deeds of the Nicolaitans,
which I also hate. He who has an ear, let him hear what the
Spirit says to the churches. To him who overcomes I will give
to eat from the tree of life, which is in the midst of the
Paradise of God" (Revelation 2:2-7).**

Jesus knows us and He knows our works. Here at Ephesus,
Jesus gives witness to what He sees the condition of the church to
be. Jesus knows their works, labor and patience. He praises the
church for turning away from evil and the influence of false apostles and the teaching of the Nicolaitans. The church is zealous for
good works and truth, yet Jesus sees that there is something lack-
ing–their first love. It must be our love for God that motivates and
drives the works of a true Christian. Without this love, truth
becomes formal and fruitless. This is the condition that threatens
the first century church. The church must, through grace, overcome this condition to one day eat from the tree of life in the
earth made new. Today Christ calls to us through this letter. We
must fall in love with Jesus anew every day, and learn of Him and
talk with Him through Bible study and prayer. We need a continu-
al 'first love' experience with Jesus.

The Seven Churches – The Church at Smyrna

**"I know your works, tribulation, and poverty (but you are
rich); and I know the blasphemy of those who say they are
Jews and are not, but are a synagogue of Satan. Do not fear
any of those things which you are about to suffer. Indeed, the
devil is about to throw some of you into prison, that you may
be tested, and you will have tribulation ten days. Be faithful**

until death, and I will give you the crown of life. He, who has an ear, let him hear what the Spirit says to the churches. He who overcomes shall not be hurt by the second death" (Revelation 2:9-11).

The Church at Smyrna, by outward appearance with its poverty, tribulation and suffering, would seem to have been abandoned by God. Yet here, Jesus gives comfort to the church. Things are not as they appear. In poverty they can know the riches of God's love for them. In persecution they can find peace by knowing that Jesus is with them and that a crown of eternal life awaits them.

In chapter three of the Old Testament book of Daniel, there is a story of persecution. In this story, three young Hebrew men, because they were faithful to God, were thrown into a fiery furnace. Although knowing that God could save them, they were willing to die for their faith. Within the furnace, the three young men stood unharmed, and standing with them was the Son of God. God will be with the faithful in their trials of life, in fact it is then that He often seems the closest.

God has promised that our trials will not be more than we can bear when trusting in Him. The trials of life are only for a short time in relationship to the eternal life that awaits us. And even if we suffer the first death of sleep in the grave, Christ assures us that just as He was dead and came to life, we who are faithful will also. We will not suffer the second death or eternal death in the lake of fire described in Revelation chapter 20.

At this point in our study, we need to take a slight detour and spend a moment looking at another important topic that is repeated and expanded throughout the book of Revelation. This deals with the question of who is a 'true Jew'. Here in the message to Smyrna there are those who say they are Jews but are not. In fact, their house of worship is actually a synagogue of Satan.

"I know the blasphemy of those who say they are Jews and are not, but are a synagogue of Satan" (Revelation 2:9).

Jesus once told a group of Jews that their father was the devil. These Jews thought that they were sons of God because they were descendants of Abraham, but because they would not let the words of truth from Jesus into their hearts, Jesus said this:

"You are of your father the devil, and the desires of your father you want to do...He who is of God hears God's words; therefore, you do not hear, because you are not of God" (John 8:44, 47).

It is those who have put their faith and trust in Jesus, and that hear and follow His word, that are now the true Jews of the New Testament.

Before we get back to Revelation let's explore this topic a little deeper.

The Jewish nation of the Old Testament had been a chosen people of God. As descendants of Abraham and holders of truth and faith in the God of creation, they were a blessed nation. Despite this, time and time again the people turned away from God into idolatry. Finally, their worship became legalistic and with cold formality centered on righteousness by works (the idea of saving oneself by trying to do good works). In chapter nine of Daniel, a prophecy concerning the Jewish nation was given. In this prophecy, a final time period was allotted to the Jews to, shall we say, 'get their act together'. During this prophecy the time of the coming messiah was given. If as a nation they would not accept Him, the blessings would be withdrawn and given to another. This is known as the seventy-week prophecy, it began like this:

"Seventy weeks are determined for your people and for your holy city, to finish the transgression, to make an end of sins, to make reconciliation for iniquity, to bring in everlasting righteousness, to seal up vision and prophecy, and to anoint the Most Holy" (Daniel 9:24).

Because in Bible prophecy a prophetic day is equal to a literal year, this seventy week prophecy is actually a 490-year prophecy. The day for a year principle occurs several times in scripture. First seen in the book of Numbers, the prophecy concerned Israel's refusal to enter the promised land of Canaan after their exodus from Egypt. After forty days of spying out the land, it was reported that because of the strength of the people it would be impossible for Israel to take possession. As punishment for the peoples' lack of faith they were sentenced to wonder in the desert 40 years, a year for each day of disbelief.

"According to the number of the days in which you spied out the land, forty days, for each day you shall bear your guilt one year, namely forty years, and you shall know My rejection" (Numbers 14:34).

Also from the book of Ezekiel, the prophet was to lie on his side facing toward Israel and then toward Judah the number of days designated by God to symbolize the number of years of their iniquity and to prophecy the coming siege by its enemies:

"For I have laid on you the years of their iniquity, according to the number of the days, three hundred and ninety days; so you shall bear the iniquity of the house of Israel. And when you have completed them, lie again on your right side; then you shall bear the iniquity of the house of Judah forty days. I have laid on you a day for each year" (Ezekiel 4:5-6).

Jesus Himself used the day for a year principal. Six months into His ministry, He foretold of the remaining three years.

"And He said to them, 'Go, tell that fox, Behold, I cast out demons and perform cures today and tomorrow, and the third day I shall be perfected. Nevertheless I must journey today, tomorrow, and the day following; for it cannot be that a prophet should perish outside of Jerusalem.'" (Luke 13:32-33).

Several times throughout Scripture the day for a year principle is used. This has been recognized for centuries and used by Bible scholars to correctly interpret these time prophecies.

The seventy-week prophecy of Daniel chapter nine was to begin at the command or decree to restore sovereignty to Israel and to rebuild Jerusalem (which had been destroyed by king Nebuchadnezzar almost a century before). Hundreds of years before its fulfillment, and embedded within the seventy-week prophecy, lay details of a time prophecy concerning Jesus coming as the Messiah. This incredible prophecy deserves a closer look.

After the decree to rebuild and restore Jerusalem (in the 7th year of Artaxerxes described in Ezra chapter 7), 483 years would go by until the messiah would be anointed. We know from historical evidence that it was in the fall of the year 457 B.C., that the decree was carried out. The first 'seven weeks' or literal 49 years would be for the rebuilding of Jerusalem. This would be followed by '62 weeks' or an additional 434 years. A total of '69 weeks' or using the day for a year principal, 483 years, would expire before the messiah would come. Adding 483 years to 457 B.C., brings us to the fall of the year 27 A.D. It was at that very time (in the fifteenth year of Tiberius Caesar-Luke 3:1), that Jesus was baptized and anointed by the Holy Spirit to begin His ministry. According to the prophecy, the Messiah would confirm the covenant for the final week or final 7 years of the 490-year prophecy. In the middle of the final seven years, the Messiah would be cut off or die, and would at His death bring an end to the sacrificial system.

"And after the sixty-two weeks Messiah shall be cut off, but not for Himself...he shall confirm a covenant with many for one week; but in the middle of the week He shall bring an end to sacrifice and offering" (Daniel 9:26-27).

*It should be noted here that this prophecy is given in a unique language and style for the book of Daniel. Unlike the Hebrew that most of the book of Daniel is written in, it is written in Aramaic poetic verse with a meter of AB - A'B'- A"B" etc... the verses speaking of the messiah (A) alternate with the prophecy of Jerusalem and its rebuilding and then final destruction by Rome (B). Let's separate the two prophecies:

Those that speak of the Messiah (meter A):

"Until Messiah the Prince, there shall be seven weeks and sixty two weeks" (Daniel 9:25).

"...And after the sixty-two weeks Messiah shall be cut off, but not for Himself" (Daniel (9:26).

"...Then He shall confirm a covenant with many for one week; but in the middle of the week He shall bring an end to sacrifice and offering" (Daniel 9:27).

Now those that speak of the rebuilding of Jerusalem and later its destruction by Rome (meter B):

"The street shall be built again, and the wall, even in troublesome times" (Daniel 9:25).

"...And the people of the prince [Rome] who is to come shall destroy the city and the sanctuary. The end of it shall be with a flood, and till the end of the war desolations are determined" (Daniel 9:26).

"...And on the wing of abominations shall be one who makes desolate, even until the consummation, which is determined, is poured out on the desolate" (Daniel 9:27)"

Jesus even spoke of this prophecy of Rome as yet future to His day.

"Therefore when you see the 'abomination of desolation,' spoken of by Daniel the prophet, standing in the holy place [area surrounding the walls of Jerusalem- see Nehemiah 13:19-22]...then let those who are in Judea flee to the mountains" (Matthew 24:15-16).

When in 70 A.D. Roman armies surrounded the walls of Jerusalem, all the Christians inside the city, because of Jesus prophecy, left and were not destroyed with the Jews when Rome attacked.

Jesus' ministry lasted three and a half years before He was put to death on the cross in the spring of 31 A.D. At His death (in the middle of the last 7 years of the 490-year prophecy), the veil within the temple was torn from top to bottom by an angel, signifying the end of the earthly sacrificial system (Mark 15:37-38). The true Lamb of God was dying, not for Himself but for the sins of the world. For another three and a half years the apostles spread the gospel among the Jews to confirm the covenant. Although many accepted Jesus as the messiah, most did not, including the priesthood and leaders of the Jewish nation. Exactly on time, at the close of the 70-week prophecy, God sent the gospel to the gentiles. In 34 A.D., at the time of the stoning of Stephen by the Jews (Acts chapter 7), Saul was called by Jesus to take the gospel of the new covenant to the gentiles. Of course, Saul changed his name to Paul and the rest is history.

The Jewish nation had sealed their final rejection of the Messiah. Their probation was over and now the new covenant spiritual nation of the Christian church was born. It would inherit the promises of God given to those who follow Him and keep His commandments. To be a 'real Jew' is, in a spiritual sense, a condition of the heart; it's not a matter of nationality. Paul puts it like this:

"For he is not a Jew who is one outwardly, nor is that circumcision which is outward in the flesh; but he is a Jew who is one inwardly, and circumcision is that of the heart, in the Spirit, and not in the letter; whose praise is not from men but from God" (Romans 2:28-29).

And to the Galatians he had this to say:

"For you are all sons of God through faith in Christ Jesus. For as many of you as were baptized into Christ have put on Christ. There is neither Jew nor Greek, there is neither slave nor free, there is neither male nor female; for you are all one in Christ Jesus. And if you are Christ's, then you are Abraham's seed, and heirs according to the promise" (Galatians 3:26-29).

26

You see, to be a true Jew is not by genetics, but by faith. If we believe in Jesus as the Son of God, and that He through the Holy Spirit will live in us to help us do His will, then we are spiritual Jews. As spiritual Jews, then spiritual sons of Abraham, and as sons of Abraham then heir to all the promises God made to his descendents. This includes a New Jerusalem built not by man, but by God himself.

"And he carried me away in the Spirit to a great and high mountain, and showed me the great city, the holy Jerusalem, descending out of heaven from God" (Revelation 21:10).

This city has been the hope of God's faithful, from all ages.

"These [saints] all died in faith, not having received the promises, but having seen them afar off were assured of them, embraced them, and confessed that they were strangers and pilgrims on the earth...But now they desire a better [country], that is a heavenly country. Therefore God is not ashamed to be called their God, for He has prepared a city for them" (Hebrews 11:13-16).

As you can see, true 'Jews' are all those, regardless of race, who hear and follow the words of Jesus-the words of God. These true Jews put their hopes in heaven and in the New Jerusalem.

Now let's go back to Revelation.

In Smyrna, the true Jews were those followers of Christ who were being persecuted for righteousness sake. These faithful would represent the future persecuted church of the second and third century (also including the 10 years [10 prophetic days] of the Diocletian persecution from 303-313 A.D.). Amidst outward despair they too would need to put their hopes in the heavenly city that God had prepared for them. And, we today should put our faith in Jesus and our hopes in heaven. Earth will bring disappointments and suffering; and, to the faithful, persecution and trials. Yet, we can live with peace in our hearts, trusting in God that one day we will live with Him in that great heavenly city.

The Seven Churches – The Church in Pergamos

"I know your works, and where you dwell, where Satan's throne is. And you hold fast to My name, and did not deny My faith even in the days in which Antipas was My faithful martyr, who was killed among you, where Satan dwells. But I have a few things against you, because you have there those who hold the doctrine of Balaam, who taught Balak to put a stumbling block before the children of Israel, to eat things sacrificed to idols, and to commit sexual immorality. Thus you also have those who hold the doctrine of the Nicolaitans, which thing I hate. Repent, or else I will come to you quickly and will fight against them with the sword of My mouth. He who has an ear, let him hear what the Spirit says to the churches. To him who overcomes I will give some of the hidden manna to eat. And I will give him a white stone, and on the stone a new name written which no one knows except him who receives it" (Revelation 2:12-17).

As a result of man's fall into sin, the dominion over the earth was passed to Satan. He became the prince of this earth and the power behind paganism, pagan kingdoms, and apostate religions.

"...You once walked according to the course of this world, according to the prince of the power of the air, the spirit who now works in the sons of disobedience..." (Ephesians 2:2).

Satan is the unseen author and authority in everything that is false and evil. Working in and through evil men, He seeks to establish earthly systems that are in opposition to God and His people. This brings trials and persecution to the faithful. So it was in Pergamos, where pagan law had established emperor worship.

The true followers of Christ, because of God's law, could not partake in idol worship or have other gods above the true God of creation. This brought persecution to the church and even martyrdom to a few such as Antipas. There was, however, compromise within the church of Pergamos. Like the Nicolaitans, some were justifying pagan worship practices.

In the Book of Numbers beginning in chapter 22, we read of the story of Balak and Balaam. Within this story is a clue to understand the message to Pergamos.

Balak was a pagan king of the Moabites who, for fear of destruction by the Israelites, sent for the prophet Balaam. Balaam had once been a true prophet but was now a false prophet and instrument of Satan. Balak had desired Balaam to come and place a curse upon Israel so that their armies could be defeated. However, when Balaam arrived all that would come out of his mouth were blessings upon the children of Israel. Not once, but four times Balaam prophesied blessing upon Israel.

Since God would not allow Balaam to curse His people, Balaam taught Balak the secret to gaining power over the Israelites. He knew that by tempting the Israelites to compromise their faith, and leading them into sexual immorality and idol worship, Israel would loose the power of God's blessing and become vulnerable. These sad words are written concerning Israel:

"Then Israel remained in Acacia Grove, and the people began to commit harlotry with the women of Moab. They invited the people to the sacrifices of their gods, and the people ate and bowed down to their gods" (Numbers 25:1).

Here, within the church of Pergamos, Satan is using the doctrine of Balaam to seduce some to compromise with the pagan practices of the city. They were eating things sacrificed to idols and committing sexual immorality. It is only by following the straight teaching of the word of God and staying close to Jesus that we are able to stay true to Him. Those who do will find truth and a deeper peace.

In John chapter 6, Jesus likened the word of God to bread, and Himself to the manna which fell in the wilderness during the 40 years of wondering by the Israelite nation. Some of this manna was placed inside the Ark of the Covenant in the most holy place of the sanctuary. This was the hidden manna of the earthly sanctuary. In like fashion, those who will follow the truth given them, will find deeper and deeper revelations from the hidden manna of truth that comes from the throne of God which is in heaven. Sadly, those who compromise truth with error will ultimately loose the conviction of the truth they once had.

Jesus promises to those who overcome, a new name. In the Bible, names were chosen to represent character. Here, in the message to Pergamos, Jesus is linking truth with character. Doctrine is important. If we follow Jesus in truth He has promised us a new character and new heart. In fact, this is the new covenant promise.

"I will put My laws in their mind and write them on their hearts; and I will be their God, and they shall be My people" (Hebrews 8:10).

Pergamos is symbolic of the fourth and fifth century church. During this time, truth would be compromised and mixed with error and elements of paganism. Also, there would be some who would remain faithful to Jesus and others who would, through compromise, bring false teaching into the church. This would be a sad era, as darkness began to envelop the organized church and its teachings.

We too must be very careful not to allow compromise in our spiritual experience. Often, Christians create their own comfortable form of religion by picking and choosing those doctrines or practices that are to their liking. Also, because of a relative ignorance of scripture, false teachings (adapted from pagan beliefs or tradition) are taught as Christian doctrine. The call of Jesus to Pergamos is a call to us today. We cannot have Christ and the world. We cannot mix truth with lies. Choose this day whom you will serve.

Roger Miller, M.D.

The Seven Churches – The Church at Thyatira

"I know your works, love, service, faith, and your patience; and as for your works, the last are more than the first. Nevertheless I have a few things against you, because you allow that woman Jezebel, who calls herself a prophetess, to teach and beguile My servants to commit sexual immorality and to eat things sacrificed to idols. And I gave her time to repent of her sexual immorality, and she did not repent. Indeed I will cast her into a sickbed, and those who commit adultery with her into great tribulation, unless they repent of their deeds. And I will kill her children with death. And all the churches shall know that I am He who searches the minds and hearts. And I will give to each one of you according to your works. But to you I say, and to the rest in Thyatira, as many as do not have this doctrine, and who have not known the depths of Satan, as they call them, I will put on you no other burden. But hold fast what you have till I come. And he who overcomes, and keeps My works until the end, to him I will give power over the nations- *'He shall rule them with a rod of iron; As the potter's vessels shall be broken to pieces'* as I also have received from My Father; and I will give him the morning star. He who has an ear let him hear what the Spirit says to the churches" (Revelation 2:18-29).

At Thyatira there had been division within the church over doctrine. There was a remnant or small group that had held true to the faith and in patient, loving service, had grown in grace and good works. Of course these are the works that come from allowing the Holy Spirit to take control of our life and produce His works of righteousness in us. These are works of faith or fruit of the Spirit that give evidence that we have a saving relationship with Jesus. Just as fruit on a tree does not make the tree alive but is evidence that the tree is alive, so also are the works of faith. They are not of our own ability; they are a gift from God that

31

comes by faith and by trusting in Him. We cannot take credit that we have produced them, it is God alone who can produce truly good works. These types of grace-driven works are spoken of in Ephesians.

"For by grace you have been saved through faith, and that not of yourselves; it is the gift of God, not of [your] works, least anyone should boast. For we are His workmanship, created in Christ Jesus for [His] good works, which God prepared before-hand that we should walk in them" (Ephesians 2:8-10).

Jesus has promised to those who through faith in Him produce this type of works, He will make to be rulers with Him as kings and priests in the new heavens and new earth. Regretfully, most at Thyatira had been led into false doctrine by false leaders and false prophets. One such false prophetess was Jezebel. It was no accident that her name was the same as one of the most notorious and evil false prophetess in Old Testament history.

First mentioned in 1 Kings 16:31, Jezebel was the daughter of Ethbaal, king of the Sidonians. She was a pagan princess and worshiper of the false god, Baal. Unfortunately, because of apostasy in the northern kingdom of Israel, King Ahab had taken Jezebel for his wife. Through her evil and idolatress influence, the people of Israel declined to a new low of sexual immorality and idol worship. Many opportunities were given for Jezebel to repent of her evil ways, but she would not. Finally, she was killed by her own people and thrown to the dogs in the streets of Israel. Her daughter, also evil, suffered a similar fate.

Prophetically, the church at Thyatira represents the great apostasy that would come to the future church. This was also foretold by the apostle Paul in a letter to the church at Thessalonica. Before the second coming of Christ, there would be a falling away from truth that would reveal the man of sin or lawlessness.

"Let no one deceive you by any means; for that Day [the coming of our Lord Jesus Christ vs.1] will not come unless the falling

away comes first, and the man of sin is revealed, the son of perdition" (2 Thessalonians 2:3).

We will have much more to say about this 'man of sin' in future chapters. This apostasy within the church, because of false doctrine from false prophets and the mixing of truth with pagan ideas, represents the church from the fifth through the fifteenth centuries. During this time, great errors came to be believed as truth, and darkness settled upon the church and its teachings. In spite of this Dark Age, there was a faithful remnant that held true to the word of God despite persecution from the unfaithful church.

Is there darkness in your faith? Are your beliefs only from the word of God or are some from the teachings and traditions of man? Is there a 'Jezebel' in your church? The message to us through the church at Thyatira is to repent and follow God and do His will. It is the only path to true happiness and eternal life. Will you follow Him?

Revelation Chapter 3

The Seven Churches – The Church at Sardis

"I know your works, that you have a name that you are alive, but you are dead. Be watchful, and strengthen the things which remain, that are ready to die, for I have not found your works perfect before God. Remember therefore how you have received and heard; hold fast and repent. Therefore if you will not watch, I will come upon you as a thief, and you will not know what hour I will come upon you. You have a few names even in Sardis who have not defiled their garments; and they shall walk with Me in white, for they are worthy. He who overcomes shall be clothed in white garments, and I will not blot out his name from the Book of Life; but I will confess his

name before My Father and before His angels. He who has an ear, let him hear what the Spirit says to the churches" (Revelation 3:1-6).

It is interesting that Jesus keeps coming back to works in His messages to the churches and especially here at Sardis. For a moment, let's take a little detour and look at what the Bible has to say about our 'works' and their importance.

Most Christians think that works do not matter. This is not so according to Jesus.

It is by your works that you will be judged. Jesus had this to say:

"For the Son of Man will come in the glory of His Father with His angels, and then He will reward each according to his works" (Matthew 16:27).

Notice this verse from Ecclesiastes.

"For God will bring every work into judgment, including every secret thing, whether it is good or whether it is evil" (Ecclesiastes 12:14).

Also in 2 Corinthians Paul had this to say.

"For we must all appear before the judgment seat of Christ, that each one may receive the things done in the body, according to what he has done, whether good or bad" (2 Corinthians 5:10).

And again in Romans:

"for not the hearers of the law are just in the sight of God, but the doers of the law will be justified...in the day when God will judge the secrets of men by Jesus Christ..." (Romans 2:13,16).

And again, from Jesus in Revelation we read:

"And behold, I am coming quickly, and My reward is with Me, to give to every one according to his work" (Revelation 22:12).

Paul says we are justified by faith alone and not of works (Rom. 3:28).

James says:

"You see then that a man is justified by works, and not by faith only" (James 2: 24).

Wow, what a contradiction. Or is it?

I believe this confusion between works and faith may need further study.

It all comes down to how you define 'works'. Let me explain.

Paul often used the word 'works' as those things that a person would do to try to make oneself good and to earn the right to one day be a citizen of heaven. He knew that man, because of the sin problem, could never do this. Man could never undo all the sin of his past and no matter how hard he tried could never perfectly keep God's law in the future. Anything that man would do without God would be messed up by sin. Even if we look good on the outside, on the inside our heart, mind, and motives, are not pure but rather selfish and evil.

Paul knew that we must look outside ourselves to God and find supernatural help. We need God's power of grace to overcome this problem. He understood and taught that only through the Spirit of God could we stop doing these polluted works, and start doing the truly good works of Jesus (works of faith). In fact, Paul knew that, unless we stopped doing these works of the flesh, as he called them, we were doomed to eternal death. It is only through the power and grace of the Spirit of God that this is possible.

"For if you live according to the flesh you will die; but if by the Spirit you put to death the deeds of the body, you will live. For as many as are led by the Spirit of God, these are the sons of God"(Romans 8:13-14).

That is why Jesus told Nicodemas that He must be born again.

"Most assuredly, I say to you, unless one is born again, he cannot see the kingdom of God"(John 3:3).

When we are born the first time by our mother, we are born unable to do good works. There is a problem with us at our very core. We are born with defective, if you please, 'software' and 'hardware'. We cannot do anything that is not corrupted by sin.

Good news! God has provided a way out. We must be born again, and this time by the Spirit. For our past record of sin, He offers forgiveness by replacing it with the perfect record of Jesus. This is grace, a free gift to those who will ask. For our future, He promises to send His Spirit to live in us and give us heavenly strength to overcome the dominion of sin in our life. This also is grace and a free gift to those who will receive Him into their hearts. Even Satan cannot stop this, because God's power to transform a life is stronger than genetics or Satan's power to ruin one.

"You are of God, little children, and have overcome them, because He who is in you is greater than he who is in the world" (1 John 4:4).

Now, the works that a truly born again (by the Spirit) Christian does through the power of the Holy Spirit are good works, works of faith. This faith in God's power to forgive us and to cleanse us from sin is spoken of in 1 John.

"If we confess our sins, He is faithful and just to forgive us our sins and to cleanse us from all unrighteousness" (1 John 1:9).

James also understood that it was only through faith in God that we could do good works. He also knew that the good works were evidence of this faith. Faith that produces good works is alive—living faith. Therefore, if we say we have faith yet do not have good works, our faith is dead.

"But do you want to know, O foolish man, that faith without works is dead...For as the body without the spirit [breath] is dead, so faith without works is dead also" (James 2:20, 26).

We now see that Paul and James are in perfect agreement.

Let's revisit, for a moment, the fruit tree illustration. If a fruit tree bears good fruit then we know that it is alive and not dead. The fruit on the tree is not what makes the tree alive but is only evidence that there is life in the tree. A dead tree, or bad tree, cannot bear good fruit.

It is the same way with the spiritual life. If we are connected to Jesus, the true vine and the good tree, then we will bear good fruit. By this fruit, people (and as we will see later, the court of heaven) will be able to judge that we are alive in Christ. It is not the fruit or good works that makes us alive only proof that we are alive. If we say we are connected to Christ yet do not bear good fruit, this is an indication that we are not really connected but are just a dead branch or a bad tree. We may be full of empty Christian words, but we will have no good fruit.

"Even so, every good tree bears good fruit, but a bad tree bears bad fruit. A good tree cannot bear bad fruit, nor can a bad tree bear good fruit. Every tree that does not bear good fruit is cut down and thrown into the fire. Therefore by their fruits you will know them" (Matthew 7:17-20).

"Abide in Me, and I in you. As the branch cannot bear fruit of itself, unless it abides in the vine, neither can you, unless you abide in Me. I am the vine, you are the branches. He who abides in Me, and I in him, bears much fruit; for without Me you can do nothing. If anyone does not abide in Me, he is cast out as a branch and is withered; and they gather them and throw them into the fire, and they are burned" (John 15:4-6).

As you can see, works (true works of faith, God's works) are very important and reveal who is in control of our life. If we trust in ourselves, no matter how good we think we are or how we may look to others, we will produce works that are corrupted by self-ishness (bad fruit). Jesus sees our works and warns us of their danger if they are not from Him. If we continue in this path, these works of ours will testify that we did not have a saving relationship with Jesus. The true gospel call is to repent of these works and through a vital connection with Jesus, produce His works of righteousness. Now, let's get back to the church at Sardis.

The church at Sardis, by saying they were Christians, should show that they were alive in Christ by bearing good fruit. Yet they were dead. Their works were not the works of God through the Spirit. They were content to do their own works. All of these works could not show them saved and could not bear witness to a transformation of their character. Their works were like filthy clothing* hanging on them as a testament to their dead faith. Isaiah puts it like this:

"But we are all like an unclean thing, and all our righteousness are like filthy rags" (Isaiah 64:6).

Clothing in scripture is often symbolic for works. First seen in Genesis, Adam and Eve through their own works tried to cover their nakedness (sin) with fig leaf garments. But it was God who made them coverings of skins (likely the first sacrificial lambs). He was teaching them, that only His works could cover their sins. Many times throughout scripture this symbolism is used, in fact, Jesus used it many times Himself. There will be more on this in the message to the church of Laodicea.

Jesus has promised to the church at Sardis that if they will have the good works of the Spirit of God they will be clothed in white. This is figurative for the pure good works that come through a living faith and trust in Jesus.

This church represents the church of the 16th and 17th centuries. This was a time when Christians were in name, but not in deeds. Roots of truth from the Protestant Reformation had begun to grow but were soon corrupted by hate, philosophy and rising secularism. This church age failed to maintain the vital connection between faith and works. Most believed that only a profession of faith with the lips was necessary for salvation. True faith however, is not about lip service it is about life service! They failed to understand the message to the churches in Revelation.

There was, however, as always a faithful few–the remnant, which because of their knowledge of the word of God and the guidance of the Spirit of Truth, produce the good fruit of Jesus. This living faith that produces good works is the requirement for having your name retained in the Book of Life. Those whose names remain in this book will be judged faithful and at last have eternal life with Jesus.

The Seven Churches – The Church at Philadelphia

"I know your works. See, I have set before you an open door, and no one can shut it; for you have a little strength, have kept My word, and have not denied My name. Indeed I will make those of the synagogue of Satan, who say they are Jews and are not, but lie-indeed I will make them come and worship before your feet, and to know that I have loved you. Because you have kept My command to persevere, I also will keep you from the hour of trial which shall come upon the whole world, to test those who dwell on the earth. Behold, I come quickly! Hold fast what you have, that no one may take your crown. He who overcomes, I will make him a pillar in the temple of my God, and he shall go out no more. And I will write on him the name of My God and the name of the city of My God, the New Jerusalem, which comes down out of heaven from My God. And I will write on him My new name. He who has an ear, let him hear what the Spirit says to the churches" (Revelation 3:8-13).

Jesus has no disapproval of the church in Philadelphia. By His authority, Jesus had provided occasion for the church to enter into revival and reformation. Taking full opportunity of the doors God had opened before them, the church was faithful in their mission of preserving truth and spreading the gospel. Despite opposition, they used what spiritual strength they had (living up to the truth they had), and did not deny Christ. Jesus promises that one day those who oppose truth and turn from God and His church, will come to justice. They will see that those who they have ridiculed and scorned were actually the true friends and sons of God. Jesus promises, because these faithful have confessed Him before man, at their time of trial He will not forsake them but provide the way of deliverance. Jesus said these words while on earth.

"Therefore whoever confesses Me before men, him I will also confess before My Father who is in heaven" (Matthew 10:32).

In the Bible, the body of believers comprising the church is sometimes likened to a building. With Jesus as the cornerstone and the apostles and prophets the foundation, the members of the church are referred to as its walls and pillars. Pillars would represent those providing great support for the church and its truth. The collective building would be the habitation of God through His Spirit. We read in Ephesians concerning those who were joining the church:

"Now, therefore, you are no longer strangers and foreigners, but fellow citizens with the saints and members of the household of God, having been built on the foundation of the apostles and prophets, Jesus Christ Himself being the chief cornerstone, in whom the whole building, being fitted together, grows into a holy temple in the Lord, in whom you also are being built together for a habitation of God in the Spirit" (Ephesians 2:19-22).

To those who are faithful as pillars in the church and upholders of truth, Jesus promises that they will also be pillars or members in the sanctuary of heaven. There at last to live forever with Jesus; eternally identified as His children with His name (character) and heirs of His kingdom the New Jerusalem in the new earth.

With a rally cry of affirmation, Jesus says to the Church at Philadelphia:

"Behold, I come quickly! Hold fast what you have, that no one may take your crown" (Revelation 3:11).

Like the Church of Philadelphia, the Church of the 18th and 19th Century experienced revival and reformation. As the printed scriptures became more widely available and God's Spirit opened doors of opportunity, great interest was shown throughout the world in fully recovering the lost apostolic truths of the first century and understanding the prophecies of Daniel and Revelation. Jesus was reforming His truths within His people. These would be the people who would give the final call of the everlasting gospel to the whole world before His second coming. Speaking prophetically of this time, Jesus states:

"And this gospel of the kingdom will be preached in all the world as a witness to all the nations, and then the end will come" (Matthew 24:14).

And in Revelation:

"Then I saw another angel flying in the midst of heaven, having the everlasting gospel to preach to those who dwell on the earth–to every nation, tribe, tongue, and people" (Revelation 14:6).

During these final moments of earth's history, Jesus is calling us to follow Him in truth and to be a witness for Him in the world. He is saying to you and me:

"Go therefore and make disciples of all the nations, baptizing them in the name of the Father and of the Son and of the Holy Spirit, teaching them to observe all things that I have commanded you; and lo, I am with you always, even to the end of the age" (Matthew 28:19-20).

The Seven Churches – The Church of the Laodiceans

"I know your works, that you are neither cold nor hot, I could wish you were cold or hot. So then, because you are lukewarm, and neither cold nor hot, I will spew you out of My

mouth. Because you say, 'I am rich, have become wealthy, and have need of nothing'–and do not know that you are wretched, miserable, poor, blind, and naked–I counsel you to buy from Me gold refined in the fire, that you may be rich; and white garments, that you may be clothed, that the shame of your nakedness may not be revealed; and anoint your eyes with eye salve, that you may see. As many as I love, I rebuke and chasten. Therefore be zealous and repent. Behold, I stand at the door and knock. If anyone hears My voice and opens the door, I will come in to him and dine with him, and he with Me. To him who overcomes, I will grant to sit with Me on My throne, as I also overcame and sat down with My Father on His throne. He who has an ear, let him hear what the Spirit says to the churches" (Revelation 3:15-22).**

The Laodiceans are in the most dangerous position of any of the churches. Spiritually blinded to their true condition, they feel no need of the Holy Spirit. They believe themselves to be rich spiritually yet they are poor and blind when seen through the eyes of Christ. In this condition, the church is very hard to awaken and reach. Like the ancient prophet of old, Jesus asks the church:

"...choose for yourselves this day whom you will serve..." (Joshua 24:15).

We are either fully for God (hot!), or we are against Him (cold!); there is no middle ground. Either we fully surrender to His will, or our will will destroy us. There is a danger in becoming complacent and lukewarm, and like the church at Laodicea slumber in our spiritual warfare.

Similar to the ten sleeping virgins representing the church in Matthew chapter 25, Jesus is giving a wake up call for them to see their true condition. Jesus offers all that the Church needs, the untarnashable character of refined pure gold earned through persevering faith in times of trial, and the white garments of good works that are not of our own effort but can only come through complete surrender to God and through the power of His Spirit. Through the spiritual vision of the Holy Spirit we will know truth and see our true condition. Because of His love for the church and those in it, He is pictured here knocking at the heart's door, waiting to be invited in and bring all these good things.

Overcoming this stupor is vital to be included as part of the kingdom of God. We must, through His Spirit, be alive and zealous for Christ. No indifferent or half-hearted effort will suffice.

This is the condition we find in most of the churches of the 20th and 21st centuries, the churches of today. Only part willing to follow Jesus and only in those things that are agreeable to themselves, the church is now found in this slumber and lukewarm condition. The good news is that before Jesus comes back, the faithful will awaken. From all denominations will come those who are willing to follow Jesus all the way. They will invite Him into their hearts and totally surrender their will to His. They will enlighten the world with the everlasting gospel and rediscovered Bible truths. They will prepare to rule with Jesus.

Will you be a part of this group who answers the knocking of Jesus? Will you let Him in your heart and have fellowship with Him? Are you willing to partake of His golden character, His works of righteousness, and His spiritual vision?

This is the last church; the final call to be a part of His coming Kingdom and to rein with Him in the new heavens and the new earth.

Chapter 3
The Heavenly Sanctuary
Revelation Chapter 4 through Chapter 8:1

"To him who overcomes, I will grant to sit with Me on My throne, as I also overcame and sat down with My Father on His throne" (Revelation 3:21).

Revelation Chapter 4

"After these things I looked, and behold, a door standing open in heaven. And the first voice which I heard was like a trumpet speaking with me, saying, "Come up here, and I will show you things which must take place after this." Immediately I was in the Spirit; and behold, a throne set in heaven, and One sat on the throne" (Revelation 4:1-2).

Chapter four opens before us one of the most majestic scenes found in the book of Revelation. We are about to take a visionary journey through an opened portal into heaven. By looking through the prophetic eyes of John, we see into the very heart of the universe, the throne room of God, the heavenly sanctuary.

The heavenly sanctuary was figuratively represented on earth by the sanctuary of the ancient Hebrew nation. God Himself gave the pattern or blueprints for this sanctuary, which are recorded in the book of Exodus. First built to be a mobile tent structure, and later a permanent structure by King Solomon, this sanctuary gives us clues in understanding the heavenly one.

Surrounded by a courtyard, which contained an altar for the lamb sacrifice and the laver of water for ceremonial washings, the sanctuary building itself contained two compartments. The two rooms were separated by a veil or curtain and were known as the

Holy and Most Holy Place. Within the Holy Place, which was the first room to be entered from the courtyard, was the seven-branched lamp stand called the menorah. This held seven lamps of fire, which gave light within the Holy Place. Also contained in the Holy Place were the table of showbread and the altar of incense.

Within the Most Holy Place, behind the veil, was the Ark of the Covenant containing the Ten Commandments. This was placed in the exact geometric center of the room. The presence of God would appear above the ark upon the mercy seat. Overshadowing the mercy seat were the images of cherubim angels. There were two such angels represented in the mobile sanctuary and later four within Solomon's temple.

As mentioned earlier in our studies, this earthly sanctuary was intended to teach Israel God's plan of salvation. The Lamb sacrifice represented Christ. The laver and its water were symbols of the washing and purification brought about by the gospel and faith in Jesus. Because of its large size in the court of Solomon's Temple, it was known as the 'Sea of Solomon.'

As a visual portal into the future, those who are being washed and cleansed from sin on the earth are reflected and seen standing above the 'Sea of Glass' that is before the throne in the heavenly temple. These are they who will be redeemed from the earth at Christ return and will literally stand before His throne in heaven.

The seven lamps were symbols of the Holy Spirit in heaven. Through Christ and His church, the Spirit of God would be a light of truth in all the world.

The table of showbread was symbolic for the word of God. According to John chapter one, Jesus was the word of God that became flesh. In John chapter six this Word (Jesus), is the bread of life that comes down out of heaven.

"For the bread of God is He who comes down from heaven and gives life to the world" (John 6:33).

It was at the altar of incense, like a communication portal, where the prayers of the saints would metaphorically rise from the earth to heaven. The Ark of the Covenant was the symbol of the very throne of God's mercy, which is founded upon his unchanging law of love, the Ten Commandments (the first four express our love for God and the last six our love for our fellow man).

The images John saw in this vision of the heavenly sanctuary were so bright and dazzling that He could only begin to describe their brilliance and colors. Using the medium of precious jewels, he paints a picture filled with radiant greens and reds. Sitting upon the throne was the form of God Himself surrounded by all the colors of the rainbow. The throne was full of light; in it was no darkness at all.

"God is light and in Him is no darkness at all" (1 John 1:5).

The concentric arrangement of the sanctuary has God's throne at its very center. Like 'wheels within wheels', with God's throne as the hub, revolved the throne room. In front of the throne were the seven lamps of fire, which are the seven Spirits of God. Here the Holy Spirit is seen as seven flames, symbolizing the completeness and perfection of His work of illumination.

Next, there was a sea with water as clear and smooth as crystal glass. Later, in chapter 15 of Revelation, the redeemed are seen standing before the throne on this sea. Standing near and surrounding the throne, are the symbolic depiction of the four living creatures that were full of spiritual vision. With the strength of a lion, the sacrificial servitude of a calf, with intelligence and discernment of a man, and the executive judgment and speed of an eagle, this exulted order of heavenly creatures serve at the throne itself.

Like the cherubim of the earthly sanctuary, they overshadow the very seat of God. It is one of these whose name is Gabriel. And sadly, Satan before his fall into sin was one of the inner circle of created beings. In a circle surrounding the throne of God, the Seven Spirits, and the four living creatures, are twenty-four thrones on which were seated the twenty-four elders. With Enoch, Moses and Elijah, they sit as a select few who have been taken alive or resurrected from the earth to fill these seats of honor around the throne.

In a larger circle surrounding the 24 thrones, was a spectacular gathering of on-looking angels numbering ten thousand times ten thousand, and thousands of thousands. In this place of worship is heard a hymn of praise:

"You are worthy, O lord, to receive glory and honor and power; for You created all things, and by Your will they exist and were created" (Revelation 4:11).

From the innermost circle to the outer wreaths of angels, the attention of all now focuses upon the symbolic figure standing at the right hand of God. This figure is the Son of Man. At his death, Stephen, the first Christian martyr, had seen a similar vision recorded in Acts.

"Look! I see the heavens opened and the Son of Man standing at the right hand of God!" (Acts 7:56).

This figure represents Christ. As the Son of Man and the Son of God, He is both the seed and offspring from the lineage of Judah and the root or origin of King David. He is described here as a lamb with blood as though it had been slain. This is symbolic of Jesus, the Lamb of God, who was sacrificed for our sins and our rebellion. Because a lamb or beast of the earth is used here in Bible prophecy to describe Jesus, He would here also represent His kingdom. Let's explore this symbolism of the kingdom of Christ further.

In Bible prophecy a beast represents a kingdom. This symbolism is used in Daniel chapters seven and eight. Daniel chapter seven describes the kingdoms of the earth from the time of Babylon to the second coming of Jesus. A lion represented Babylon; a bear, Media-Persia; a leopard, Greece; and a fourth, dragon-like beast, Rome. In chapter eight of Daniel it is a ram that represents Media-Persia (Daniel 8:20), and a he-goat that represents Greece (Daniel 8:21).

Jesus, the lamb, as the head of the body of the church on earth, represents His spiritual kingdom. Because He has prevailed on earth against sin, Christ is now heir not only to the spiritual but also to the physical kingdom that will inherit the earth after His second coming.

The chain of authority upon the earth, leading up to Christ kingdom, is clearly described in the dream given to King Nebuchadnezzar and found in Daniel chapter 2. Much like chapter seven and eight of Daniel, the order of future earthly kingdoms are given.

Nebuchadnezzar had been considering what would become of the great kingdom of Babylon he had built. In a dream, God showed him the future kingdoms of this world. By using a symbolic statue, Nebuchadnezzar saw the future of his kingdom and the kingdoms that would follow.

First there was the statue's head of gold, which symbolized Babylon itself. Next, was its chest of silver, the kingdom that would follow Babylon, the Media-Persia Empire (we see this fulfilled in Daniel chapter five). To follow the Media-Persians, would be the kingdom of Greece represented by its thighs of brass. The fourth kingdom, the images legs of iron, was the kingdom of Rome. There would not be a fifth united kingdom to rule the earth; rather the fourth kingdom—Rome would be divided into smaller kingdoms (what we see in the nations of Europe today). These kingdoms were described as the statue's feet of iron and clay.

According to the vision, it would be at the time of these smaller kingdoms that the kingdom of Christ would be set up upon the earth. Symbolized as a large rock, which would strike the image in the feet, it would come to the earth and destroy the kingdoms

of man and establish itself as the only remaining victorious kingdom. This kingdom of Christ would then fill the whole earth and
stand forever as an everlasting kingdom.

*"And in the days of these kings [of the divided kingdom of
Rome] the God of heaven will set up a kingdom which shall never
be destroyed; and the kingdom shall not be left to other people; it
shall break in pieces and consume all these kingdoms, and it shall
stand forever" (Daniel 2:44).*

Revelation Chapter 5

Because of His victory over sin, Jesus is seen here in
Revelation ready to receive the authority and dominion over His
kingdom. This scene is also described in the book of Daniel.

*"I was watching in the night visions, and behold, One like the
Son of Man, coming with the clouds of heaven! He came to the
Ancient of Days, and they brought Him near before Him. Then to
Him was given dominion and glory and a kingdom, that all peoples, nations, and languages should serve Him. His dominion is
an everlasting dominion, which shall not pass away, and His
kingdom the one which shall not be destroyed" (Daniel 7:13-14).*

In Revelation, the kingdom of Jesus is described as having
seven horns–figurative of its perfect strength. It also has seven
eyes, which symbolically represent its perfect spiritual illumination. This is the light Jesus sends by His Spirit to the churches
upon the earth. Jesus as the head and representative of His kingdom, stands at the right hand of God, ready to receive a sealed
scroll or book from, 'He who sat on the throne.'

The clue to understanding this scene is found within the
Jewish coronation ceremony of a new king. Here the king to be
crowned is handed a scroll of the book of the law, the book of

Deuteronomy. Because of his spiritual leadership responsibilities and authority as king, he would open the scroll and then make a personal copy of the text. He would then teach all in Israel what was contained within the book. This included the law of God as given in His commandments (repeated in Deuteronomy from Exodus chapter 20) and blessings promised to those who would obey as well as curses and plagues that would come to those who did not. The duties of the new king are described as follows.

"And it shall be, when he sits on the throne of his kingdom, that he shall write for himself a copy of this law in a book, from the one before the priests, the Levites. And it shall be with him, and he shall read it all the days of his life, that he may learn to fear the Lord his God and be careful to observe all the words of this law and these statutes, that his heart may not be lifted above his brethren, that he may not turn aside from the commandment to the right hand or to the left, and that he may prolong his days in his kingdom, he and his children in the midst of Israel" (Deuteronomy 17:18-20).

We see this carried out at the coronation of king Joash.

"And he brought out the king's son, put the crown on him, and gave him the Testimony; they made him king and anointed him, and they clapped their hands and said, "Long live the king!" (2 Kings 11:12).

And when king Josiah found the book of the law in the house of the Lord, he read to the people and made a covenant to keep His commandments.

"...and he read in their hearing all the words of the Book of the Covenant which had been found in the house of the Lord...and made a covenant before the Lord, to follow the Lord and to keep His commandments..." (2 Kings 23:2-3).

At this heavenly coronation and enthronement ceremony of Jesus, He is declared worthy to be king, to regain rulership of the earth and to represent the church as a faithful High Priest of the heavenly sanctuary. The 24 elders declare:

"You are worthy to take the scroll, and to open its seals; for You were slain, and have redeemed us to God by Your blood out of every tribe and tongue and people and nation, and have made us kings and priests to our God; and we shall reign on the earth" (Revelation 5: 9, 10).

This scroll or book that Jesus receives from the Father is comparable to the book of the Law received by the kings of Old Testament Israel. It fact, it is the very content of the book of Revelation. As Deuteronomy foretold future blessings to those who would be faithful, it also gave warning to those who would be unfaithful. In a way, Revelation is the New Testament, New Covenant equivalent to the book of Deuteronomy. Received from God and 'rewritten' as prophetic messages to the churches from our King, Jesus Christ. It is the future of His church on earth; it exalts the law of God and speaks of blessings for those who will keep His Law as well as curses and plagues to those who will not.

Revelation Chapter 6

In chapter six of Revelation, Jesus begins to unseal the scroll. Because He has been found worthy, He alone has the honor and authority to uncover the future of the church and of His kingdom. In clearly symbolic language, the seals of Revelation 6-8:1, visually unfold the prophetic application of the seven churches we studied earlier. They tell the future of the church from the first century until the return of Jesus; a future of faithfulness amid darkness and apostasy. A future, although bleak at times, with a final triumphant and victorious church that will finally establish the eternal kingdom of Christ.

Next, we read what John saw as the first seal was opened.

"And I looked, and behold, a white horse. And he who sat on it had a bow; and a crown was given to him, and he went out conquering and to conquer" (Revelation 6:2).

Within the first four seals, the church's future is symbolized as horses and their riders. Similar language is used in Old Testament passages from Zechariah concerning prophecies of the church. Corresponding to the first century church, this rider of the first seal is a symbol of victory and truth, a symbol of Christ. Christ is also seen riding a white horse at His victorious return to this earth.

"Then I saw heaven opened, and behold, a white horse. And He who sat on him was called Faithful and True, and in righteousness He judges and makes war" (Revelation 19:11).

With the unbridled power of the Spirit, the 1st century gospel truth went forth victorious, spreading throughout the then known world. Paul has this to say:

"...because of the hope which is laid up for you in heaven, of which you heard before in the word of the truth of the gospel, which has come to you, as it has also in all the world..." (Colossians 1:5, 6).

Wherever the true gospel is preached, persecution will follow. As we saw in the message to the church of Smyrna, persecution soon fell heavy upon the church.

"When He opened the second seal, I heard the second living creature saying, "Come and see". And another horse, fiery red, went out. And it was granted to the one who sat on it to take peace from the earth, and that people should kill one another; and there was given to him a great sword" (Revelation 6:4).

Seen here as a red horse symbolic for blood and war, representing both the outward persecution and inward betrayal that would try the 2nd and 3rd century church. However, because of the rising political popularity of Christianity from the early 4th century through the 5th century, truth was soon compromised with pagan beliefs. Like the church at Pergamos, there was a seduction of the church by the practices of heathen religions. Soon, truth became scarce with only a remnant of the church remaining faithful to Jesus.

"When He opened the third seal, I heard the third living creature say, "Come and see". And I looked, and behold, a black horse, and he who sat on it had a pair of scales in his hand. And I heard a voice in the midst of the four living creatures saying, "a quart of wheat for a denarius, and three quarts of barley for a denarius; and do not harm the oil and the wine" (Revelation 6:5, 6).

The black horse and its rider represent the presence of spiritual darkness. From the Old Testament books of Leviticus and Ezekiel, we find a clue for the meaning of the pair of scales found in the hand of the rider.

"When I have cut off your supply of bread, ten women shall bake your bread in one oven, and they shall bring back to you your bread by weight, and you shall eat and not be satisfied" (Leviticus 26:26).

"Moreover He said to me, "Son of man, surely I will cut off the supply of bread in Jerusalem; they shall eat bread by weight and with anxiety, and shall drink water by measure and with dread, that they may lack bread and water, and be dismayed with one another, and waste away because of their iniquity" (Ezekiel 4:16-17).

In times of plenty there was no need to carefully weigh out rations of bread and water; in times of famine, scales would become necessary. Yet, here in the third seal where the grains for bread are used to symbolize the word of God, the famine is for truth and God's word. We hear this type of famine expressed in the prophecy of Amos.

"Behold, the days are coming, says the Lord God, that I will send a famine on the land not a famine of bread, nor a thirst for water, but of hearing the words of the Lord" (Amos 8:11).

Because of this famine of truth and light, darkness settles upon the church and truth becomes scarce. It is only by sacrifice and great cost (all of a days wages–a denarius) that the word of God can be found. Yet, even in these times, the oil and the wine, symbolic for the Holy Spirit and the gospel of God's salvation through the blood of Jesus, can still be found for those who truly seek them.

From darkness and apostasy we move to the fourth seal, Death.

"When He opened the fourth seal, I heard the voice of the fourth living creature saying, "Come and see." And I looked, and behold, a pale horse. And the name of him who sat on it was Death, and Hades followed with him. And power was given to them over a fourth of the earth, to kill with sword, with hunger, with death, and by the beasts of the earth" (Revelation 6:7-8).

On the heels of spiritual decay and darkness, the church itself now became a persecuting power of death and destruction. With the pale lifeless color of death this symbolic horse and its rider typifies the church of the 6th through 15th centuries. As there was compromise with pagan beliefs and truth was replaced by the traditions of man, so did the very lifeblood of the church drain from its body.

Intolerant of those who opposed its doctrine and system of worship, it turned upon the faithful throughout its centuries to kill and persecute those who would not violate conscience. For over one thousand years, the apostate church would seem to prevail against the true saints of God, and like the church of Thyatira, 'Jezebel' as symbolic queen would rein and bring an evil and idolatress influence. Like Jezebel and Ahab in Israel of old, false religion and civil authority would join in an unholy union. This age would produce the largest number of Christian martyrs in the history of the church. Known as the Dark Ages, it still stands today infamous for its crimes against humanity. This period of spiritual darkness had also been foretold in the prophecies of Daniel. Once again, to find the clues we need, we turn to this book.

In the vision of chapter 7, Daniel described four beasts coming up out of the sea. These were symbolic of kingdoms that would arise from the sea of humanity. The first, like a lion with wings would represent Babylon just as the statue's head of gold in Daniel chapter 2. The second beast was like a bear. This kingdom would be the Media-Persian Empire that would follow Babylon's rule, again seen in the dream of the image as its chest of silver. A third leopard-like beast would follow; like the thighs of brass it would represent the kingdom of Greece. A fourth kingdom depicted as a dreadful, terrible and strong beast with iron teeth, would follow Greece. This was the iron kingdom of the statue in chapter 2- the kingdom of Rome. If you will remember, a single fifth kingdom did not follow Rome; but rather its strength was divided into smaller kingdoms like the ten toes of the feet of iron and clay. Here in chapter seven this division is symbolized by ten horns growing out of the head of the fourth beast. Horns are symbolic for strength of the kingdom and divisions of this strength (this definition is later given by Gabriel in the vision of chapter eight).

Of particular interest, in chapter seven's vision was an additional little horn that grew out of the head of the fourth beast. This power would arise out of Rome after the time of Rome's division into ten smaller powers. In the process of immerging out of the head of the fourth beast, it would destroy or uproot three of the original ten horns or kingdoms.

"...it [the fourth beast] had ten horns. I was considering the horns, and there was another horn, a little one, coming up among them, before whom three of the first horns were plucked out by the

roots. And there, in this horn, were eyes like the eyes of a man, and a mouth speaking pompous words" (Daniel 7:7-8).

Sometime after Rome was divided among the ten Germanic tribes of Europe in the 5th century, would arise this little horn power. From the seventh chapter of Daniel, let's list some of its characteristics to see if we can unlock its identity.

-In rising to power, it would destroy three of the original ten kingdoms from their 'roots' (vs. 8)

-Its eyes were like the eyes of a man (vs. 8)

-It had a mouth speaking pompous words against God (vs. 8, 25)

-It would make war and persecute the saints of the Most High and for awhile would prevail against them (vs. 21, 25)

-The saints would be given into his hand for a time (1 year) and times (2 years) and half a time (one-half year). [From Daniel 4:16, a time is equal to one year. Therefore, this represents three and one-half years of prophetic time. This would equal 42 months or with 30 days in a Jewish month, 1260 prophetic days—1260 years in actual literal time.]

-It shall intend to change (God's) times and (God's) law (vs. 25)

-And, it would be destroyed by God as a result of the Judgment (vs. 11, 26)

I think, in our study so far, we have enough clues to solve the mystery of the little horn.

This kingdom would arise out of divided Rome in the 5th century and would destroy three kingdoms as it came into power. As a power, its eyes or spiritual eyesight was not of God, but as man sees things. With its mouth it would speak against God, pompous and blasphemous words. How does a kingdom speak? Through its decrees and laws. So also, this power would make decrees and proclamations against God's law and His established order of time. By doing so, it would exalt itself above God. This power would, for over one thousand years (1260 years), persecute and make war against God's true saints.

For over five centuries, and by almost all major Protestant reformers, this power has been understood to be the apostate church of Rome and its rise as the Roman Catholic Church, which came to power between 476 A.D. and 538 A.D. Through its influence, three Germanic kingdoms were eradicated from the earth. This opened the way for it to receive its civil authority from (what was left of) Rome in 538 A.D.; thus uniting church and state and beginning the 1260-year prophecy of its reign.

During its reign, pagan idolatry and teachings (such as life after death and hell as a literal place of torture within the earth), were canonized into church doctrine. God's laws concerning idols and God's set times of the weekly seventh-day Sabbath were changed by church decree. This apostate system would claim the power to forgive sins by being god on earth- speaking pompous and blasphemous words.

All those who would not bow the knee to Papal authority met the fate of persecution and death. Some estimates place the number of martyrs during this time at nearly 60 million. In 1798 under Napoleon, the Roman Catholic Church would seem to come to its end and thus conclude its 1260 year reign. At the same time it was coming to its end, a great religious revival throughout the protestant churches occurred.

As we will see in the prophecies of Revelation chapter 12 and 13, this apostate church power (although seemingly dead at the end of the 18th century), would come to life again before the second coming of Christ. It should be remembered that the prophecies are speaking of kingdoms, church systems, and organizations not individuals. God has His faithful in all churches, which He is now calling together before He comes back to earth.

"And other sheep I have which are not of this fold; them

also I must bring, and they will hear My voice; and there will be one flock and one shepherd" (John 10:16).

And in Revelation 18:4, speaking of this apostate system (here symbolically called Babylon):

"Come out of her [Babylon], My people, least you share in her sins, and lest you receive of her plagues."

Thus fulfills the fourth seal and the prophetic application of the messages to the churches of Thyatira, Sardis and Philadelphia.

As a result of the persecution and death of the fourth seal, the cry of the martyrs of the fifth seal would be heard.

"When He opened the fifth seal, I saw under the altar the souls of those who had been slain for the word of God and for the testimony which they held. And they cried with a loud voice, saying, 'How long, O Lord, holy and true, until You judge and avenge our blood on those who dwell on the earth?' And a white robe was given to each of them; and it was said to them that they should rest a little while longer, until both the number of their fellow servants and their brethren, who would be killed as they were, was completed" (Revelation 6:9-11).

Here, seen at the base of the altar, are the souls of those who had been martyrs for Christ. This symbolic language comes from the practice of pouring out the blood of the sacrificial animal at the base of the altar in the service of the sanctuary (Ex. 29:12, Leviticus 4:18). Jesus, the Lamb, was martyred for His faith and those who are killed for the faith of Jesus are identified with Him. In the book of Genesis, after Cain had murdered his brother Abel God had this to say:

"The voice of your brother's blood cries out to Me from the ground"(Genesis 4:10).

Like Abel's innocent, martyred blood symbolically cried from the ground for justice, here in the fifth seal are heard the cries of the faithful asking how long before their blood would be avenged

Jesus, figuratively, answers with an assurance to them of their white robes of righteousness but states that they will have to remain resting in the grave until all is complete. A time is coming when all injustice will meet the court of heaven and only righteousness will prevail. When Jesus comes the second time, He will execute judgment according to what each has done.

"Do not be deceived, God is not mocked; for whatever a man sows, that he will also reap. For he who sows to his flesh will of the flesh reap corruption, but he who sows to the Spirit will of the Spirit reap everlasting life. And let us not grow weary while doing good, for in due season we shall reap if we do not lose heart" *(Galatians 6:7-9).*

It is also true that even in this life there is a level of justice that we have to face.

"Even as I have seen, those who plow iniquity and sow trouble reap the same" *(Job 4:8).*

"He who sows iniquity will reap sorrow…" *(Proverbs 22:8).*

In the book of Revelation, Jesus will answer the cry of the saints. We will see in chapters 8 and 9, judgments that have come, and will come, to all those who persecute God's faithful people. These are the warning trumpets of coming final judgments. In chapters 15 through 18 these final judgments fall upon the wicked as the seven last plagues and the fall of figurative Babylon. In chapter 19 the second coming of Christ brings judgment to all false systems of worship, and finally in chapter 20 at the end of the millennium, the ultimate destruction of all those who practice evil and have turned away from God's salvation.

As an answer to the cries of the fifth seal, the sixth seal gives a first glimpse at the judgments that will come at Christ's second coming.

"I looked when He opened the sixth seal, and behold, there was a great earthquake; and the sun became black as sack-

cloth of hair, and the moon become like blood. And the stars of heaven fell to the earth, as a fig tree drops its late figs when it is shaken by a mighty wind. Then the sky receded as a scroll when it is rolled up, and every mountain and island was moved out of its place. And the kings of the earth, the great men, the rich men, the commanders, the mighty men, every slave and every free man, hid themselves in the caves and in the rocks of the mountains, and said to the mountains and rocks, 'Fall on us and hide us from the face of Him who sits on the throne and from the wrath of the Lamb! For the great day of His wrath has come, and who is able to stand?'" (Revelation 6: 12-17).

From the symbolic language of the first five seals, there is an obvious shift into a literal depiction of the second coming of Christ. Despite how things may appear and how wickedness seams to flourish, in the end Jesus and His people will be victorious. Only those who have chosen their own path, the path of sin, will want to hide from Jesus when He comes. Those who have repeatedly rejected the call of the Spirit through their conscience will hide in terror as they hear this same voice coming from the lips of Jesus. This scene of the sixth seal is not a secret or local event but universal in its consequence and all will be affected. Preceded by unnatural declarations from the sun, moon and stars, even the heavens will be shaken. While this is a time of strife and horror for the lost, this is a time of victory for the saved.

"For the Lord Himself will descend from heaven with a shout, with the voice of an archangel, and with the trumpet of God. And the dead in Christ will rise first. Then we who are alive and remain shall be caught up together with them in the clouds to meet the Lord in the air. And thus we shall always be with the Lord" (1 Thessalonians 4:16-17).

This seal ends with a question, "For the great day of His wrath has come, and who is able to stand?" Chapter seven of Revelation gives us the answer, the 144 thousand.

Revelation Chapter 7

Many have heard of the 144,000 described in Revelation chapter seven. Let's discover, using our keys to Bible prophecy, who these people really are. First of all, this group is mentioned in two places in the book of Revelation; chapter seven, where we are studying now, and chapter fourteen. We will use both chapters to discover their true identity.

Chapter seven opens with a scene of four angels standing at the four corners or four directions of the earth. They are holding or restraining the winds of strife that are about to come upon the earth. This includes the physical earth itself, the people of the earth which are represented by the seas (see-Rev.17:15), as well as the church represented by the trees (see Psalms.1:3, 52:8, 92:12-14; Isaiah 61:3; Jeremiah 11:15-17, 17:7-8; Ezekiel 20:46-48). This apparently is the conflict that will come upon the earth prior to the second coming of Jesus described later in the sixth trumpet. The reason they have not let go of the 'winds' is given in verse three.

"Do not harm the earth, the sea, or the trees till we have sealed the servants of our God on their foreheads."

The next verse states that John heard the number of those who were sealed. The number was 144 thousand, 12 thousand from each of the 12 tribes of the children of Israel. The list in order is as follows:

Judah

Reuben

Gad

Asher

Naphtali

Manasseh

Simeon

Levi

Issachar

Zebulun

Joseph

Benjamin

Those who will be able to stand at the great day of God's wrath are those who have the seal from God in their foreheads. What could this mean? The clue is found in Ezekiel chapter nine. This chapter describes what was to happen as judgment and destruction fell upon Jerusalem. In this vision we see behind the scenes as God tells His angels what to do before the evil and wicked people of the city are destroyed.

"Go through the midst of the city, through the midst of Jerusalem, and put a mark on the foreheads of the men who sigh and cry over all the abominations that are done within it" *(Ezekiel 9:4).*

"To the others He said in my hearing, "Go after him through the city and kill...but do not come near anyone on whom is the mark; and begin at My sanctuary" *(Ezekiel 9:5-6).*

Those with the mark would stand or survive the judgment that was about to befall Jerusalem. These were the faithful of Israel, those who were sad for the sin of its people.

Another clue, before we put this all together, concerns where this mark from Ezekiel and the seal from Revelation is placed. For this we go to the book of Exodus and read this concerning Aaron the high priest of Israel.

"You shall also make a plate of pure gold and engrave on it, like the engraving of a signet: HOLINESS TO THE LORD. And

you shall put it on a blue cord that it may be on the turban; it shall be on the front of the turban. So it shall be on Aaron's forehead" (Exodus 28:36-38).

I think you are beginning to get the idea of how important our keys to prophecy are.

Here we see a sign or mark of Aaron's commitment to God. Placing it over his forehead was symbolic of his mind and thoughts. This was a sign that He had dedicated his mind and heart to the service of God, to be of holy service to God.

Likewise, the seal or mark of Revelation is symbolic of those who have given their life in service to God to follow Him and keep His commandments. Their minds and characters are being washed clean by following Jesus and allowing the Holy Spirit to have control of their lives. Those who have made this commitment will stand through earth's final trials before Jesus comes. As we have already seen from previous chapters, true Jews of the true Israel of God are all those who have made this dedication and given their minds and hearts to Jesus. This mark or seal in the mind of God's people is in contrast with the unholy mark of Satan and the beast of Revelation chapter 13 that we will study later.

There are several points about the number 144 thousand that should be noted. First, the number is given (in the original language) in somewhat of a peculiar way. Instead of 144,000, it is given as 144 thousand or 144 units of 1000 each. The clue to this is found again in the Old Testament. When Israel was preparing for war, fighting men of each tribe would be subdivided in smaller units of 1000. This is seen many times in Scripture.

"A thousand from each tribe of all the tribes of Israel you shall send to the war" (Numbers 31:4).

In fact, this unit of a thousand was the number that a captain would command:

"...to the captain of their thousand..." (1 Samuel 17:18).

"Therefore Saul removed him from his presence, and made him his captain over a thousand..." (1 Samuel 18:13).

As for the number 144 we find the following:

In Scripture the number twelve represents the church. In the Old Testament there were 12 tribes from the 12 sons of Israel. In the New Testament, there were twelve disciples of spiritual Israel, the church of the new covenant. In fact, to keep this number and because of its importance, another was chosen to replace Judas.

"Therefore, of these men who have accompanied us all the time that the Lord Jesus went in and out among us...one of these must become a witness with us of His resurrection...and they cast their lots, and the lot fell on Matthias. And he was numbered with the eleven apostles" (Acts 1:21, 22, and 26).

The woman who represents the true church described in Revelation chapter twelve, has 12 stars (12 apostles) as a garland on her head. Even in the New Jerusalem of chapter 21, there are 12 gates and 12 foundations numbered for the 12 tribes and 12 apostles. Also its wall measured 144 cubits; of course 12 squared or 12 times 12 equal 144.

You see, the number 144 thousand is symbolic of completeness of the church; completeness of the church that is prepared for battle, a battle of good against evil. This is a spiritual battle of the heart and mind. In Revelation there are two choices; either we stand for Christ and receive His mark or seal (the true Israel of God), or we take the side of Satan and receive his mark.

Further symbolic characteristics of the 144 thousand described in chapter seven and chapter 14 are:

- The list of tribes in Revelation chapter seven is a unique list in scripture. This is the only list that begins with Judah. Jesus is the lion of the tribe of Judah, thus Judah is now in a preeminent position.

- The Old Testament tribe of Dan is missing from the list, as is one of the sons of Joseph, Ephraim (later in Israel's history, the tribe of Joseph was replaced with two tribes representing his sons). These two tribes of Dan and Ephraim were notorious in the history of Israel as the leaders in apostasy, rebellion and idol worship as well as betrayers of their brethren. Since names represent character, these are not included because there is no inheritance in heaven for those who retain these traits of sin.

- John had only heard the number of those who were sealed. When, in verse nine, he actually sees this group he says the following:

"After these things I looked, and behold, a great multitude which no one could number, of all nations..." (Revelation 7:9).

Here, John sees that this group is larger than 144,000 and that they are from all nations. In chapter 14, the 144 thousand are described as having God's name written on their foreheads. As we have seen, a name in scripture often has meaning in relationship to one's character. This symbolized that they will have the character of God in their minds. This is the fulfillment of the new covenant that God promised to spiritual Israel in Jeremiah 31:31-34 and again repeated in Hebrews 8:10-12.

"...I will put My laws in their mind and write them on their hearts..." (Hebrews 8:10-12).

Also, in chapter 14 verse 4, the 144 thousand are stated to, "not [be] defiled with women, for they are virgins..." In a spiritual, symbolic sense, these are faithful to their betrothed husband, Jesus.

"...For I have betrothed you to one husband, that I may present you as a chaste virgin to Christ" (2 Corinthians 11:2).

Jesus also used symbolic virgins to represent the church in the parable of the ten virgins told in Matthew chapter 25.

As you can see, there is much symbolism related to the 144

thousand. To summarize, this is a group of the faithful from every nation that represent the true and faithful church of spiritual Israel. These, because of their trust in God, have been partakers of the new covenant. Their minds and hearts are in harmony with God's character of His perfect law of love, His commandments. Spiritually prepared for battle, they will be able to stand through the Great Tribulation before the second coming of Christ. They rest in the grace of Jesus to wash and cleanse them from all unrighteousness and clothe them in white garments of His righteousness. These are the ones who are seen through the laver to serve before the throne of God upon the sea of glass in the heavenly sanctuary. These are the ones, with those from all ages, who are resurrected when Jesus comes; who will finally inherit the literal kingdom of Jesus and the New Jerusalem in the new earth.

"These are the ones who come out of great tribulation, and washed their robes and made them white in the blood of the Lamb. Therefore they are before the throne of God, and serve Him day and night in His temple. And He who sits on the throne will dwell among them"(Revelation 7:14-15).

Those who serve God in His spiritual kingdom will serve Him in His literal one. Would you like to be one of the 144 thousand, one of those who are able to stand? It is your choice. God has and will provide all you need to be 'counted' with the faithful.

Revelation Chapter 8

"When He opened the seventh seal, there was silence in heaven for about half an hour" (Revelation 8:1).

The seals of Revelation have opened before us the history of the church and its fall into apostasy. As a result of this apostasy, there was persecution to those who remained faithful, the faithful remnant, the true Jews of spiritual Israel. In the fifth seal, the blood of those who had died for truth is heard crying to God for justice. This justice, and the outcome of the unfaithful at the return of Jesus, are unveiled in the sixth seal.

Those who are able to survive His coming are described in chapter seven as the symbolic 144 thousand, those who have God's law written in their minds. The seventh seal of silence in heaven calls our attention to the coming judgments of all those who stand against God and His church. A clue to understand this seal is from the book of Zechariah. Just prior to a vision of a judgment scene in the court of heaven, are these words:

"Be silent, all flesh, before he Lord, for He is aroused from His holy habitation!" (Zechariah 2:13).

When God moves in His justice and executive judgments, all are commanded to be silent. Creator and judge of all, this attitude of silent respect and honor is made concerning His authority. This silence is for a short time, 'half an hour.' God will not delay when it comes time to administer justice and His movements will be rapid.

Chapter 4

The Trumpets-Beginning of Judgment

Revelation Chapter 8:2 through Chapter 11

The Trumpets of chapters 8 through 11 of Revelation are the warning judgments of the final and complete judgments that will come to all of those who oppose God and His faithful people.

Because of their highly symbolic language, the trumpets of Revelation are often misinterpreted. We must use the keys for symbolic prophetic interpretation to arrive at a correct understanding. We need to remember what we have already learned from the churches and seals of Revelation and apply that knowledge here.

Trumpets were used by ancient Israel for many purposes: as a call to worship, a call to assemble, the call to war, and as a call of alarm and warning. With no telephones, television or radios, the trumpet would make a certain sound to communicate with the people of Israel. Notice these verses from Numbers chapter 10.

"The sons of Aaron, the priests, shall blow the trumpets; and these shall be to you as an ordinance forever throughout your generations. When you go to war in your land against the enemy who oppresses you, then you shall sound an alarm with the trumpets, and you will be remembered before the Lord your God, and you will be saved from your enemies. Also in the day of your gladness, in your appointed feasts, and at the beginning of your months, you shall blow the trumpets over your burnt offerings and over the sacrifices of your peace offerings; and they shall be a memorial for you before your God: I am the Lord your God" (Numbers 10:8-10).

In fact, in the final month of the Jewish religious calendar there was a special day of sounding the trumpets; calling and warning the people to prepare for the coming Day of Atonement, the Day of Judgment.

"In the seventh month, on the first day of the month, you shall have a sabbath-rest, a memorial of blowing of trumpets, a holy convocation...Also the tenth day of this seventh month shall be the Day of Atonement. It shall be a holy convocation for you; you shall afflict your souls, and offer an offering made by fire to the Lord" (Leviticus 23:24-27).

The Day of Atonement, or Day of Judgment as it was known, was when judgment would come against sin. Through the lamb's symbolic blood and by God's mercy, the sanctuary was cleansed from the record of forgiven sin. The sins were then symbolically placed upon the head of a goat, representing Satan the author of all sin, and led into the wilderness to die. We will have much more to say about this later.

In Revelation 8:3-4 we see within the heavenly sanctuary an angel at the altar of incense. As mentioned in a previous chapter, this is where the prayers of the saints are symbolically communicated from earth to heaven. Because of the prayers of the persecuted and martyred saints, heaven acts in judgments. God knows the suffering of His people and hears their prayers. These judgments against those who oppress His people are not complete or final, but ones that call for repentance. They, however, are warnings announcing and leading up to the final judgments, plagues and destruction that will come upon those who do not repent.

"The first angel sounded: And hail and fire followed, mingled with blood, and they were thrown to the earth; and a third of the trees were burned up, and all green grass was burned up" (Revelation 8:7).

Sometimes in Old Testament scripture, judgments from God would be prophesied using these elements of hail, fire and blood. The seventh plague of the book of Exodus that fell upon the Egyptians was hail mixed with fire. Also, from the book of Ezekiel, we read this concerning the judgments of God against Gog a heathen king and enemy of Israel:

"I will call for a sword against Gog throughout all My Mountains, says the Lord God. Every man's sword will be against his brother. And I will bring him to judgment with pestilence and bloodshed; I will rain down on him, on his troops, and on the many peoples who are with him, flooding rain, great hailstones, fire, and brimstone" (Ezekiel 38:21-22).

Here in the first trumpet, we see judgments from God fall upon a third of trees and all the green grass. Trees and green grass are symbolic terms at times applied in Old Testament prophecies to God's covenant people. Jesus Himself referred, in parable, to the nation of Israel with tree illustrations: as a tree in Luke 23:31, and as a fig tree that was without fruit in Matthew 21:18-19. Even Paul, in the book of Romans, uses the cultivated olive tree to illustrate God's people. We also saw this symbolism used in chapter seven of Revelation.

During the first century it was the nation of Israel that had Jesus put to death and it was this nation that pursued and persecuted the early Christian church. This first trumpet judgment from God is against Israel. Jesus prophesied of this judgment in Matthew.

"O Jerusalem, Jerusalem, the one who kills the prophets and stones those who are sent to her! How often I wanted to gather your children together, as a hen gathers her chicks under her wings, but you were not willing! See! Your house is left to you desolate; for I say to you, you shall see Me no more till you say, 'Blessed is He who comes in the name of the Lord!'" (Matthew 23:37-39).

Their 'house' or temple no longer had the presence or blessings from God, it had been deserted. As Jesus and His disciples overlooked the city of Jerusalem from the Mount of Olives, He said this:

"Do you not see all these things? Assuredly, I say to you, not

one stone shall be left here upon another, that shall not be thrown down" (Matthew 24:2).

The nation of Israel came to the end of their covenant relationship in 34 A.D., at the conclusion of the 70-week prophecy. The new covenant relationship with spiritual Israel had begun. All that the nation of Israel had left was to wait for God's judgments against them. This first trumpet judgment was fulfilled against the nation of Israel in 70 A.D., when the Romans completely destroyed the temple and the city of Jerusalem.

Like Babylon of old had executed God's judgments hundreds of years before, Rome now executes His judgments upon the nation of Israel. However, Babylon itself eventually came to its own time of judgment, as did the Romans.

"Then the second angel sounded: And something like a great mountain burning with fire was thrown into the sea, and a third of the sea become blood; and a third of the living creatures in the sea died, and a third of the ships were destroyed" (Revelation 8:8-9).

The clue to this trumpet is found in the book of Jeremiah. In a prophecy concerning ancient Babylon and God's judgments against it.

"Behold, I am against you, O destroying mountain, who destroys all the earth, says the Lord. And I will stretch out My hand against you, roll you down from the rocks, and make you a burnt mountain...The sea has come up over Babylon; she is covered with the multitude of its waves"(Jeremiah 51:25, 42).

In symbolic language, Babylon is referred to as a mountain that would fall, burning, down into the sea. Babylon had fulfilled the divine judgments against apostate Israel, but because of their own crimes against humanity and God's people, they too would come to justice. Likewise, as we saw in the second seal, it was the Romans who persecuted the faithful during the 2nd and 3rd centuries during the prophetic time period of Smyrna. This second trumpet judgment was fulfilled against Rome during the 5th century. Through great conflict and bloodshed, it was divided into ten smaller kingdoms by the barbaric Germanic tribes of Europe.

"Then the third angel sounded: And a great star fell from heaven, burning like a torch, and it fell on a third of the rivers and on the springs of water; and the name of the star is Wormwood; and a third of the waters become wormwood; and many men died from the water, because it was made bitter" (Revelation 8:10-11).

A star in symbolic prophecy (see Rev. 1:20) represents an angel. This star or angel, once in heaven, has fallen to the earth and struck the pure water of the springs and rivers. In scripture, the water of springs and rivers represent the truth of the gospel. Often, in both Old and New Testament scriptures, this symbolism is used. Jesus used this as He talked with the woman from Samaria at Jacob's well:

"...but whoever drinks of the water that I shall give him will never thirst. But the water that I shall give him will become in him a fountain of water springing up into everlasting life" (John 4:14).

By this angel, the sweet and pure truth of the gospel is turned into a lie and made bitter like wormwood (an Old Testament symbol of God's judgment against apostasy). The final effect is death to men who drink it. It is Satan, the fallen great star, that is this author of lies and deception. In Revelation chapter twelve we read this concerning Satan:

"So the great dragon was cast out[of heaven], that serpent of old, called the Devil and Satan, who deceives the whole world; he was cast to the earth, and his angels were cast out with him" (Revelation 12:9).

As we saw in the prophetic application to the churches of Pergamos, Thyatira, and Sardis, as well as the third seal of the black horse, through Satan's influence lies would come into the church and bring compromise, darkness and a famine for truth. Spiritual death would follow to those who believe the lies and do not receive the love of the truth. Here, in the third trumpet judgment, those who are in apostasy and persecute God's faithful are given up to believe the false gospel that they preach. But in their lives it does not bring the peace and joy that only the true gospel can bring. It does not satisfy the deep needs and thirsting of their souls. The falsehoods of Satan turn into bitter disappointments and despair, and if not repented of, they will finally bring about eternal death.

As the sun brings light and life to this planet, so darkness symbolizes death. And the fourth angel sounded:

"And a third of the sun was struck, a third of the moon, and a third of the stars, so that a third of them were darkened; and a third of the day did not shine, and likewise the night" (Revelation 8:12).

The sun here represents truth and grace from Jesus Himself. His countenance was described in Revelation 1:16 like the sun shining in its strength. The moon's light is reflected from the sun. In the same way, Jesus reflects light through the prophets to His people. The stars are angels of light that bring messages of truth to His people on earth. As we will see later in chapter 12 of Revelation, a symbolic pure woman representing the church is described as standing on the moon (the prophets), clothed with the sun and with a garland of twelve stars about her head. Here, in the fourth trumpet, a third of these lights are seen as darkened. Because of Satan's influence on the church and the gospel, the illuminations from these lights are dim and obscure. As man tries to create his own religion, soon basic gospel truths are lost. As a result, man begins to follow a path that seems right but ends in darkness and death.

"There is a way which seems right to a man, but its end is the way of death" (Proverbs 14:12).

This is the condition in which we find the church of the Dark Ages. Not only was it a persecuting power, but as judgments from God, it too would reap suffering and fear under its own superstitions as well as wars, disease, and spiritual poverty. If we leave the light of truth then we are open to the judgments and consequence of sin. The final three trumpets, also known as the three woes, are about to sound.

"Woe, woe, woe to the inhabitants of the earth, because of the remaining blasts of the trumpet of the three angels who are about to sound!" (Revelation 8:13).

The 5th and 6th trumpets are given in some of the most symbolic and difficult language to understand in the book of Revelation. We will study these two trumpets together and look at the symbolism a segment at a time. Then we will put everything together for a summary.

Revelation Chapter 9

"And I saw a star fallen from heaven to the earth..." (Revelation 9:1).

We have already seen from the third trumpet that this is Satan

"... And to him was given the key to the bottomless pit" (Revelation 9:1).

God holds the ultimate authority over Satan and the fallen angels. Like in the story of Job, God has put limits upon them. But here, in the 5th and 6th trumpets, in succession these limits are withdrawn. This is the beginning of greater authority given to Satan to reveal his kingdom of darkness upon the earth- to make final war against truth and good.

"And he opened the bottomless pit, and smoke arose out of the pit like the smoke of a great furnace. And the sun and the

**air were darkened because of the smoke of the pit"
(Revelation 9:2).**

Satan is seen here opening the bottomless pit or abyss. In metaphoric language, like opening a door of opportunity, Satan begins his final works of spiritual deception. The darkness of his kingdom further dims the light of God's truth, and the efforts of the Holy Spirit, like the air we breathe, are also in part suffocated by this dark presence.

**"Then out of the smoke locusts came upon the earth..."
(Revelation 9:3).**

Locusts, often a Biblical sign of judgments from God, represent destroying agents. Here, they are symbolic of Satan's kingdom of fallen angels- the demons of darkness.

"... And to them was given power, as the scorpions of the earth have power" (Revelation 9:3).

The locusts or demons here are given power. This power and authority has been granted to them. The church has mostly turned away from God and His Spirit of truth, and here God is releasing Satan and his kingdom to demonstrate their full destructive potenial. Like serpents and scorpions of the wilderness, their only design is to bring pain, suffering and death.

"They were commanded not to harm the grass of the earth, or any green thing, or any tree, but only those men who do not have the seal of God on their foreheads" (Revelation 9:4).

Even here, as demonic activity is unleashed, God has put restrictions on Satan and access to the faithful is limited. Those who have His law of love written in their minds and hearts are protected. If we stay close to God and His truth, Satan cannot spiritually harm us. Jesus says this:

"Behold, I give you the authority to trample on serpents and scorpions, and over all the power of the enemy, and nothing shall by any means hurt you" (Luke 10:19).

Their description continues:

"And they were not given authority to kill them, but to torment them for five months. And their torment was like the torment of a scorpion when it strikes a man. In those days men will seek death and will not find it; they will desire to die, and death will flee from them" (Revelation 9:5-6).

In addition to the restriction concerning God's new covenant people, the demons are not allowed, at this time, to fully display their deadly potential. This will come in the 6th trumpet. The five months given for their plague of destruction, is a definite period of time. Like the flood of Genesis harmed the earth for five months, so these plagues of symbolic locust do theirs. Historically, there was also a time period of 150 literal years (5 prophetic months is equal to 150 literal years) between 674 A.D. and 823 A.D., where the apostate false religion of Islam, like a plague, waged physical and theological war on the Holy Roman Empire at Constantinople. There is, however, a limited duration of this 5th trumpet before the sounding of the 6th trumpet, for it is appointed to sound at a definite point in time before the second coming of Jesus. Like the affliction that comes from the sting of a scorpion, so comes the mental and physical suffering from this plague of destructive deception and pagan philosophies.

"And the shape of the locusts was like horses prepared for battle; and on their heads were crowns of something like gold, and their faces were like the faces of men. They had hair like women's hair, and their teeth were like lions' teeth. And they had breastplates like breastplates of iron, and the sound of their wings was like the sound of chariots with many horses running into battle. They had tails like scorpions, and there were stings in their tails. And their power was to hurt men five months" (Revelation 9:7-10).

Here is a list of symbolic characteristics of the demons prepared for war. This imagery is barrowed from Joel, speaking of judgments against Israel and prophetically of future events before the coming of the day of the Lord.

"What the chewing locust left, the swarming locust has eaten; what the swarming locust left, the crawling locust has eaten; and what the crawling locust left, the consuming locust has eaten...For a nation has come up against My land, strong and without number; his teeth are the teeth of a lion, and he has the fangs of a fierce lion...Blow the trumpet in Zion...For the day of the Lord is coming...a day of darkness and gloominess, a day of clouds and thick darkness...Their appearance is like the appearance of horses; and like swift steeds, so they run. With a noise like chariots over mountaintops they leap, like the noise of a flaming fire that devours the stubble, like a strong people set in battle array. Before them the people writhe in pain; all faces are drained of color. They run like mighty men, they climb the wall like men of war...the sun and moon grow dark, and the stars diminish their brightness... For the day of the Lord is great and very terrible; who can endure it?" (Joel 1:4-6; 2:1-10).

Arrayed for spiritual battle and with authority and intelligence, the demons do their work. Seeking to devour like the lion, they bring with their tails the deception of false prophets.

"Be sober, be vigilant; because your adversary the devil walks about like a roaring lion, seeking whom he may devour" (1 Peter 5:8).

And from Isaiah:

"...the prophet who teaches lies, he is the tail" (Isaiah 9:15).

"His [Satan's] tail drew a third of the stars of heaven and threw them to the earth" (Revelation 12:4).

In scripture the tail is symbolic for falsehood and deception. Like the tail of a scorpion brings pain and destruction, Satan, his demons and false prophets do the same.

"And they had as king over them the angel of the bottomless

pit, whose name in Hebrew is Abaddon, but in Greek he has the name Apollyon" (Revelation 9:11).

'*Abaddon*' in Hebrew means *destruction*, and '*Apollyon*' in Greek means *destroyer*; This is referring to Satan, the prince of darkness, the king of demons and the author of death and destruction.

Now, in the 6th trumpet, God is commanding the four angels described in chapter seven as holding back the winds of destruction, to begin to release them.

"So the four angels, who had been prepared for the hour and day and month and year, were released to kill a third of mankind" (Revelation 9:15).

This is an intensification of Satan's authority compared to the 5th trumpet. He and his demons are now allowed to kill a third of mankind, to bring spiritual death. This event is to occur at a set time.

"Now the number of the army of the horsemen was two hundred million, and I heard the number of them" (Revelation 9:16).

A great army is depicted here, but despite this, God is still in control and able to defeat.

"And thus I saw the horses in the vision: those who sat on them had breastplates of fiery red, hyacinth blue, and sulfur yellow; and the heads of the horses were like the heads of lions; and out of their mouths came fire, smoke and brimstone. By these three plagues a third of mankind was killed-by the fire and the smoke and the brimstone which came out of their mouths. For their power is in their mouth and in their tails; for their tails are like serpents, having heads; and with them they do harm" (Revelation 9:17-19).

Described here ready for spiritual battle, the demons are prepared to devour with judgments of destruction and deception. This time their work has a finished product of death-spiritual death.

Despite seeing what Satan's kingdom brings, most do not repent.

"But the rest of mankind, who were not killed by these plagues, did not repent of the works of their hands, that they should not worship demons, and idols of gold, silver, brass, stone, and wood, which can neither see nor hear nor walk; and they did not repent of their murders or their sorceries or their sexual immorality or their thefts" (Revelation 9:20-21).

Let's summarize:

As further judgments against apostasy and evil within the church, Satan is given authority to release the fury of his kingdom. Satan's host of demons, prepared for spiritual warfare to devour truth with falsehood and deception, cause even greater darkness to come upon the earth. Having authority, these warring demons bring anguish, despair and a drunken stupor upon the minds of all those who are not protected by having God's truth and laws implanted in their hearts. Because God does not take pleasure in the destruction of the wicked, this judgment is given as a call to repentance. By God's mercy, there is still time to turn to truth and be saved. As with all of Satan's lies, these additional false teachings and philosophies bring an escalation of wars, poverty, disease, destruction and the results of greed, to the earth. We see, at least in part, the fulfillment of this trumpet in the rise of the Religion of Islam through the false prophet Mohammad. Bringing even greater spiritual confusion to the earth as well as hundreds of years of great conflict, Islam has been a plague to the apostate Christian church.

As the final warning call and at the appointed time, the 6th trumpet is sounded. Before God moves in His final executive judgments and plagues against evil, He now commands the four angels, described in chapter seven, to begin to unleash the full ferocity of the destructive forces of Satan's kingdom upon humanity. Held in check until now and intensified from the 5th trumpet, the demons now have power and authority to kill.

The full ripening of the fruit of sin is now being made evident, the full cost of false religion and pagan philosophies begin to take their toll on earth and within the apostate churches. Yet, most do not repent and turn from sin.

Lies of Satan, described in previous trumpets, have done their work. Now deceived and without truth, most of mankind hold on to their false worship and materialism–following in the wide path of destruction and death. Their sins of violence, especially against the innocent, their false philosophies of paganism and new age spiritualism, their immoral societies who practice adulteries, fornications and homosexuality, and their greed that destroys the earth, are filling full their symbolic cup of iniquity.

We see partial fulfillment of this trumpet in the modern false philosophies that have been a plague of death to spiritual and moral values as well as given rise to some of the greatest world wars this planet has ever seen. These include popular humanistic views, materialism, communism and atheistic ideologies with evolution as their doctrine; as well as repackaged New Age movements of spiritualism and of pagan religions such as Hinduism and Buddhism.

Further fulfillment will come, as the greatest deceptions of Satan are about to fall upon the earth in his final attack against God's truth and his people (we will see these details expanded later in the book of Revelation). God is now preparing to act in His final phases of salvation, to destroy and eradicate sin and those who cling to sin, forever.

The seventh trumpet is about to blow. But before it sounds, Revelation unveils heaven's response to the intensified demonic activity of the 6th trumpet. God does not let Satan's war against truth go unchallenged. In the light of rekindled gospel truth, and as a final plea to mankind, God calls a people to take light and warning to the whole world as a last loud cry and plea to repent and worship the true God, the God of Creation. Although outnumbered in this war, His power is with them. Chapters 10 and 11 are the prophecy of these people.

Revelation Chapter 10

In contrast to the great fallen angel, chapter 10 introduces a mighty angel that comes down from heaven with clouds. This heavenly messenger has a rainbow on his head with a countenance like the sun. His feet are like pillars of fire. In his hand is a small open scroll or book. He is standing with one foot on land and the other on water. Lifting one hand toward heaven He proclaims in the name of He who lives forever and ever, in the name of the creator, that there should be delay no longer. He declares that the mystery of God's salvation is about to be completed at the time of the sounding of the seventh trumpet.

Again, the clue to this passage is found in the book of Daniel.

Daniel described a similar heavenly messenger in the visions of chapter 8, chapter 10 and chapter 12. In chapter 8 the messenger's voice is heard coming from over the river. In chapter 10, He is described as clothed in linen with a gold belt, with a face like lightning, and eyes of fire. In chapter 12 we read this:

"Then I heard the man clothed in linen, who was above the waters of the river, when he held up his right hand and his left hand to heaven, and swore by Him who lives forever, that it shall be for a time, times, and half a time; and when the power of the holy people has been completely shattered, all these things shall be finished. Although I heard, I did not understand. Then I said, "My Lord, what shall be the end of these things?" And he said, "Go your way, Daniel, for the words are closed up and sealed till the time of the end. "Many shall be purified, made white, and

refined, but the wicked shall do wickedly; and none of the wicked shall understand, but the wise shall understand."...But you, go your way till the end; for you shall rest, and will arise to your inheritance at the end of the days" (Daniel 12:7-13).

The heavenly messenger from the prophecies of Daniel is the same messenger we see in Revelation chapter 10. He is announcing the fulfillment of Daniel's vision. The time had come at the conclusion of the time, times and half of time, when the prophecies of Daniel were to be understood. The book was now unsealed and lying open in the messenger's hand. But what from the book of Daniel was to be understood? What was sealed until the time of the end?

A little more study and insight into the prophecies of Daniel is needed before we continue.

Let's go back to the vision of Daniel chapter eight.

As in chapters two and seven of Daniel, the succession of kingdoms upon the earth is described, from the Media-Persian Empire to the kingdom of Papal Rome, it again repeats and expands the prophecies of earth's future. From divided Greece of verse eight, verse nine shifts the focus to a little horn power and its conquest. The power is described as growing 'exceedingly great' in all directions. The language suggest that this power was even greater than that of the Media-Persian, described in verse 4 as a 'great' power, and Greek kingdoms, described in verse 8 as 'very great' power, that came before it. This little horn, as we have already seen from chapter seven of Daniel, represents Papal Rome, which grew out of the 'head' of pagan Rome. Since Papal Rome is both a civil and religious power, both its Roman-horizontal conquest of the nations and its Papal-vertical attack upon God and His true sanctuary, are described.

"And out of one of them [one of the four winds (north) from verse 8- later described as the 'King of the North' in chapter 11] came a little horn which grew exceedingly great toward the south

*toward the east, and toward the Glorious Land [west]. And it
grew up to the host of heaven; and it cast down some of the host
and some of the stars to the ground, and trampled them. He even
exalted himself as high as the Prince of the host; and by him the
daily sacrifices were taken away, and the place of His sanctuary
was cast down" (Daniel 8:9-11).*

Here, Satan is identified as working through the apostate
church-state union of Rome to attack God and His heavenly sanctuary. Of course, this is not a literal physical attack but rather a
theological attack against truth. As we have already seen from
previous chapters, this attack against truth would last for 1260
years, from 538 A.D., to 1798 A.D.

Within the prophecies of chapter eight, there is an additional
time prophecy known as the 2300-year prophecy. It is the longest
time prophecy in the Bible. This prophecy will become very
important to our understanding of the meaning of the open scroll
in the hand of the mighty angel in Revelation chapter 10.

Let's spend a few moments and study this prophecy.

In Daniel 8:13, Daniel overhears a heavenly conversation.
When asked when the conclusion of the attack by the little horn
against God and His sanctuary would be, this is the answer given:

*"For two thousand three hundred days; then the sanctuary
shall be cleansed" (Daniel 8:14).*

Using the prophetic day for a literal year principle, this
prophecy concerning the cleansing of the heavenly sanctuary
would be fulfilled at the end of 2300 years!

Now that's a long prophecy!

But when would this prophetic time clock start ticking, and
what does it mean to cleanse the heavenly sanctuary?

We find one of the answers in the vision of the 70-weeks
found in chapter nine. Gabriel had explained many of the details

of the vision of chapter eight but had not explained the meaning of the 2300 days. By the end of chapter eight, Daniel was still puzzled concerning this most disturbing time prophecy concerning the sanctuary.

"I was astonished by the vision, but no one understood it" *(Daniel 8:27).*

In chapter nine, after Daniel prays for his people, Gabriel is sent to Daniel to explain how his people and the city of Jerusalem are related to the 2300 days of the prophecy. Gabriel says this:

"...I have now come forth to give you skill to understand...therefore consider the matter and understand the vision; Seventy weeks are determined for your people..." (Daniel 9:22-24).

The 70-week prophecy, concerning the final probation of Daniel's people, the nation of Israel, was 'determined' (literally meaning- *'to cut out'*) from the longer 2300-day prophecy from chapter eight. In other words, only the first 70 weeks of the 2300 days related to Daniel's people and the city of Jerusalem.

From this, we can know that the 2300-day prophecy would begin when the 70-week prophecy started. This, of course, according to Daniel 9:25, was at the decree to restore and rebuild Jerusalem in 457 B.C. With simple addition, we can find that the 2300-day, or 2300 literal year prophecy, would come to an end in 1844!

According to Daniel chapter 8, at this time there would be a restoration of truth concerning God's work on our behalf in the heavenly sanctuary. This understanding had been lost and distorted-'cast down' during the 1260-year rein of the apostate Roman church. At the end of this time prophecy, the full meanings of the symbolic earthly sanctuary services were then to be understood because they were soon to be fulfilled in the heavenly sanctuary. This would occur at a time known, according to Daniel chapter 12, as the 'time of the end.' At that time, knowledge would be increased and the mysteries of the book of Daniel would be unsealed and made known. The true meaning of the symbolic daily sacrifice and yearly services of the earthly sanctuary would then be understood.

For centuries the apostate church had claimed the power and authority to forgive sin. The daily sacrifice of the earthly sanctuary service, when rightly understood, taught that it was God alone through the sacrifice of His Son that can forgive sin. This forgiveness does not now require the payment of a lamb or the intercession of an earthly priest. Jesus is our High Priest and through Him we can boldly approach the throne of grace. Paul in Hebrews has this to say:

"Seeing then that we have a great High Priest who has passed through the heavens, Jesus the Son of God, let us hold fast our confession. For we do not have a High Priest who cannot sympathize with our weakness, but was in all points tempted as we are, yet without sin. Let us therefore come boldly to the throne of grace, that we may obtain mercy and find grace to help in time of need" (Hebrews 4:14-16).

Each repentant sinner, through prayer, can ask Jesus for forgiveness, and He has promised to forgive us and to cleanse us from all unrighteousness. Again from John:

"If we confess our sins, He is faithful and just to forgive us our sins and to cleanse us from all unrighteousness" (1 John 1:9).

Another mystery of Daniel's prophecies concerns the cleansing of the heavenly sanctuary found in chapter 8 vs. 14. This cleansing was to occur at the end of the 2300 years, which, we now know, was in 1844. Again, the meaning of this heavenly cleansing comes from understanding the cleansing of the earthly sanctuary on Yom Kipper or the Day of Atonement, Day of Judgment.

Symbolically, the records of forgiven sins were recorded within the earthly sanctuary. By bringing the blood of the sacrificial lamb (sin offering) into the holy place and sprinkling it upon the horns of the altar and upon the veil, the record of forgiven sins were figuratively 'written' or recorded within the sanctuary. This occurred daily throughout the year. Each year, on the 10th day in the last month of the Jewish religious calendar, there was a special day of cleansing the sanctuary from this record of sin. This day was referred to as the Day of Atonement or Day of Judgment.

This service of the earthly sanctuary is found described in Leviticus chapters 16 and 23. Once a year, on this day, the high priest would go into the Most Holy Place where the Ark of the Covenant was. This time, by placing the blood of the sacrificial lamb upon the mercy seat of the ark, he would be symbolically removing the record of sins through the forgiving grace of God. The high priest would then symbolically place the guilt of these sins upon the head of the scapegoat, representing the final placement of sin and guilt upon Satan.

In a similar way, the records of forgiven sins have been 'written' in the heavenly sanctuary. These too have been recorded and forgiven on the basis of the symbolic blood of Jesus. According to the prophecy, in the year 1844 there would begin the fulfillment of the heavenly cleansing. The record of forgiven sins would begin to be removed and forgotten. These words are found, also as a part of the promise of the new covenant:

"For I will be merciful to their unrighteousness, and their sins and their lawless deeds I will remember no more" (Hebrews 8:12; Jeremiah 31:34) .

As this evidence is investigated, those who have received forgiveness will forever have their sins removed from the books. By God's mercy, these people are to be the citizens of the New Jerusalem. From all ages of earth's history, only those whose sins are found forgiven and cleansed are retained in the book of the saved, the Book of Life. All those who failed to trust in God and receive forgiveness, must bear their own record and penalty of sin, unforgiven and uncleansed. And like Satan, they too will receive the final punishment for sin.

At the close of the 2300-year prophecy in 1844, would begin the investigation and cleansing of the records in heaven. This will reveal to the court of heaven who will be redeemed from the earth at the second coming of Jesus. This scene is described in the vision of Daniel chapter seven:

"I watched till thrones were put in place, and the Ancient of Days was seated; His garment was white as snow; and the hair of His head was like pure wool. His throne was a fiery flame, it's wheels a burning fire; a fiery stream issued and came forth from before Him. A thousand thousands ministered to Him; ten thousand times ten thousand stood before Him. The court was seated, and the books were opened" (Daniel 7:9-10).

Like the throne room coronation and enthronement of Jesus in Revelation chapter four, this investigative judgment scene is another part of the salvation plan to forever remove sin and its record from the universe.

Let's now go back to Revelation chapter 10. In verse 8 and 9, John is asked to take the open scroll from the angel and eat it. The book was sweet in John's mouth but made his stomach ache with bitterness. Then John was told that he must:

"prophesy again about many peoples, nations, tongues and kings" (Revelation 10:11).

Eating and digesting a book is clearly symbolic of the process of reading and understanding. The word of God is sometimes referred to as the bread of life that is to be eaten or read and understood. Jesus uses this reference in John chapter six. Also, this symbolism is used in the book of Ezekiel chapters two and three.

"Now when I looked, there was a hand stretched out to me; and behold, a scroll of a book was in it...Moreover He said to me,

"Son of man, eat what you find; eat this scroll, and go, speak to the house of Israel"...So I ate it, and it was in my mouth like honey in sweetness" (Ezekiel 2:9, 3:1,3).

The first understanding of the prophecies of Daniel were sweet, but later this sweet experience turned into a bitter one. John was then told to prophesy again about many people. This new message and its understanding would be based on the understanding of the sanctuary.

Revelation Chapter 11

"Then I was given a reed like a measuring rod. And the angel stood saying, "Rise and measure the temple of God, the altar, and those who worship there" (Revelation 11:1).

It would be the sanctuary and its symbolic messages that would be the basis of true understanding in the once-sealed prophecies from the book of Daniel. Revelation's prophecy, telling of this experience, is the prophecy of God calling together a remnant people who understand these truths and "measure up" by keeping them. They were to proclaim the message of the prophecies of Daniel and Revelation that were then being opened and understood at the time near the end of the 1260 and 2300 years-between 1798 and 1844.

At first, this understanding would result in a sweet experience but latter would turn bitter. Historically, this exact fulfillment occurred in the early to mid 1800's. At that time, as the understanding of Daniel's prophecies were coming to light, there was an initial misunderstanding concerning the cleansing of the sanctuary described in Daniel 8:14. The interpretation held that the earth was the sanctuary and its cleansing was by fire at the second coming of Jesus. There was a movement, lead in the United States by William Miller, as well as in multiple other countries by many others, proclaiming that the second coming of Jesus to this earth would occur in the year 1844 at the end of the 2300-year prophecy.

This teaching became so popular in the United States, it was estimated that one in four Americans had heard this proclamation and many believed it to be true. Of course, Jesus did not come in 1844, and to many, the once sweet experience turned bitter. It was shortly after this disappointment, under the guidance of the Holy Spirit and by a careful study of the symbols of the earthly sanctuary, that the true understanding of the cleansing of the heavenly sanctuary became evident.

As we have already learned, this was a cleansing of the record of forgiven sins of those who have given their life to trusting in God. This investigation of the record within the heavenly sanctuary had begun at the time of the end. When complete, it would be followed by the literal second coming of Jesus.

The understandings of Bible prophecy along with reformed apostolic Bible truths were to be proclaimed by a people as the everlasting gospel to the whole world and then the end would come. These Bible truths included: the literal, visible, pre-millennial second coming of Jesus to the earth, the true Sabbath of the fourth commandment, the truth concerning the 'sleep like' state of death, and the finality of sin in the lake of fire. These people were to be God's answer to Satan's attacks of the 6th trumpet.

This movement of prophetic destiny is known today as the Seventh-day Adventists. From all denominations, people who have discovered Bible truth and understand the prophecies of Daniel and Revelation have come together to take this last loud cry of the everlasting gospel to the world.

Revelation 11:2-14, gives an overview of why there was a need to reform Biblical truths and call a people to exalt the Bible above the teachings and philosophies of men. Again, reviewing and expanding the prophecies of Revelation, this section adds

detail that help us understand why modern anti-Biblical philosophies were able to gain strength as described in the 6th trumpet.

The first rein of the apostate Roman church, as we have seen,
would last for a time, times, and half of time or 1260 years from
538 to 1798 A.D. During this time, the church on earth (figuratively represented by the courtyard of the earthly sanctuary),
would be given over to the Gentile or pagan doctrines to "tread
the holy city [or God's true people] underfoot for forty-two
months." These 42 months are the same time period described in
Daniel and later in Revelation chapter 12, as the 'time, times and
half of time' (In three and one half years there are 42 months or
1260 days). Even during this time, the Bible and its truths testi-
fied against the apostate church. Through the lives of the faithful
remnant and the witness of the faithful martyrs, God spoke to
mankind to turn and repent of their evil. Even though the
Scripture would testify to, and prophesy of, these times of spiritual famine, they would do so with symbolic mourning in sack
cloth. Jesus also personified scripture when He called it a witness
that would testify for Him.

*"You search the Scriptures, for in them you think you have
eternal life; and these are they which testify of Me" (John 5:39).*

Here in Revelation, the two witnesses are the Old and New
Testament. As witnesses, both give testimony to Jesus and His
truth. Their stories tell of the true God of creation and His miracu-
lous power over it.

**"These [two witnesses] have power to shut heaven, so that no
rain falls in the days of their prophecy; and they have power
over waters to turn them to blood, and to strike the earth with
all plagues, as often as they desire" (Revelation 11:6).**

**"Now when they finish their testimony, the beast that ascends
out of the bottomless pit will make war against them, overcome them, and kill them" (Revelation 11:7).**

At the end of the 1260 years, Satan would make an attack to

'kill and destroy' Scripture. This attack has already been described in the 6th trumpet. Historically, this fulfillment started in Europe at the end of the 18th century as Christianity and the Bible came under attack by atheistic ideology particularly from the nation of France during the French revolution. Bibles were burnt and Christianity was declared dead. The pope was dethroned and sent into exile where he later died. The churches properties were taken and given to the state and the people. For three and one half literal years (three and one-half prophetic days) at the close of the 1700's, Europe celebrated the death of the Bible, the two witnesses.

"Then those from the peoples, tribes, tongues, and nations will see their dead bodies three and a half days, and not allow their dead bodies to be put into graves. And those who dwell on the earth will rejoice over them, make merry, and send gifts to one another, because these two prophets tormented those who dwell on the earth" (Revelation 11:9, 10).

As Jesus could not be held in death, so His word would come back to life. With an earthquake, God's word would be resurrected and shake the earth, as a religious revival would circle the globe. However, as described in the 6th trumpet, this period would also give rise to most modern anti-Biblical philosophies that now plague the modern world. These anti-God and anti-truth teachings have further infiltrated the church bringing additional confusion and resultant evil. They have caused, in most part, the death of morality and genuine faith in the Creator–God (even in so called Christian churches). As a result of this, the seventh trumpet announces the coming of the 'rock' kingdom of Jesus Christ.

"Then the seventh angel sounded: And there were loud voices in heaven, saying, 'The kingdoms of this world have become the kingdoms of our Lord and of His Christ, and He shall reign forever and ever!'" (Revelation 11:15).

This announcement of Christ's kingdom is followed by a proclamation of the 24 elders stating that judgment has come:

"We give You thanks, O lord God Almighty, the One who is and who was and who is to come, because You have taken Your great power and reigned. The nations were angry, and Your wrath has come, and the time of the dead, that they should be judged, and that You should reward Your servants the prophets and the saints, and those who fear Your name, small and great, and should destroy those who destroy the earth" (Revelation 11:17-18).

This Judgment, of course, begins in 1844 with the investigative phase and cleansing of the record of sin from the Heavenly Sanctuary. This scene is described in verse 19:

"Then the temple of God was opened in heaven, and the ark of His covenant was seen in His temple" (Revelation 11:19).

Only on the day of atonement was the Most Holy Place opened and the ark seen. On this heavenly Day of Atonement, the work of cleansing the sanctuary had begun in the heavenly Most Holy Place, the throne room of God.

Why is there a need for cleansing of the heavenly sanctuary? Where did sin come from and why this war on earth between good and evil?

In the next chapter, as a panoramic historic overview, we will see that there is war on earth because there was first war in heaven.

Chapter 5

The Great Controversy between Good and Evil

Revelation Chapter 12 through Chapter 14

This section of Revelation (chapters 12-14), is a snapshot overview of the conflict between God and Satan. From the beginning through its final events, this great war between good and evil is told. Set within the chiastic center of the book of Revelation, these chapters are an interlude between the now mostly historic portion of the book (ch.1-11) and its yet future prophecies. God arranged Revelation in this way with foreknowledge as to when the opening and understanding of Daniel would occur.

As we saw in the last chapter, the prophecies of this 'little book' are now open. These unsealed prophecies, at the time of the end, help link the past and yet future prophecies of Revelation. By seeing fulfillment of prophecy, the last generations are given added faith and confidence in God and His final victory over sin. We are living in that time now.

<u>Revelation Chapter 12</u>

"Now a great sign appeared in heaven; a woman clothed with the sun, with the moon under her feet, and on her head a garland of twelve stars. Then being with child, she cried out in labor and in pain to give birth. And another sign appeared in heaven: behold, a great, fiery red dragon having seven heads and ten horns, and seven diadems on his heads. His tail drew a third of the stars of heaven and threw them to the earth. And the dragon stood before the woman who was ready to give birth, to devour her Child as soon as it was born. And she

bore a male Child who was to rule all nations with a rod of iron. And her Child was caught up to God and to His throne. Then the woman fled into the wilderness, where she has a place prepared by God, that they should feed her there one thousand two hundred and sixty days" (Revelation 12:1-6).

Here, John sees a pure woman. This symbol represents the faithful church within Israel (it was through God's faithful of the nation of Israel that the promised messiah would come). She stands on the moon (prophets) and is clothed in the light of truth from God.

She is ready to give birth to the Christ. A symbolic dragon is seen ready to devour the child as soon as it is born. This dragon, representing Satan, tried to destroy Jesus during His life on earth. Although Jesus was crucified, He was victorious in His mission to defeat sin and Satan. As we saw in chapter 4 of Revelation, following the resurrection Jesus was taken to the throne of His Father in heaven to receive His kingdom and to be anointed as our High Priest of the heavenly sanctuary. Because Satan had failed in this spiritual battle against Jesus, he now pursues the faithful church, the object of Christ affection.

"Then the woman fled into the wilderness, where she has a place prepared by God, that they should feed her there one thousand two hundred and sixty days" (Revelation 12:6).

A clue to this symbolism is found in the story of Elijah during Ahab's rule of the northern kingdom of Israel. Because of the apostasy and idolatry of the kingdom, God had sent a drought for three and a half years. During this time, God took care of Elijah in the wilderness by sending food from heaven. Also, during this time there was a remnant of 7000 in Israel who remained faithful to God.

Like the prophet Elijah and the remnant that did not bow the knee to Baal, here in Revelation a remnant of the faithful is preserved. And like God fed Elijah for three and a half literal years with food from heaven, He also provided the faithful with spiritual food during these three and a half prophetic years of apostasy (1260 years). Although sometimes in obscurity, there has always been a faithful remnant. Why this war between the faithful church and Satan? Verse seven explains:

"And war broke out in heaven..." (Revelation 12:7).

The war between good and evil, between Christ and Satan, and between the faithful church and the kingdom of darkness, first began in heaven. Satan, once known as Lucifer; the light bearer, had once been a cherubim angel within the inner circle of the throne room of God. Because he become dissatisfied with his position as a created being and desired to be like God himself, he began a rebellion against the government of God.

From Isaiah we read:

"How you are fallen from heaven, O Lucifer, son of the morning! How you are cut down to the ground, you who weakened the nations! For you have said in your heart: 'I will ascend into heaven, I will exalt my throne above the stars of God; I will also sit on the mount of the congregation on the farthest sides of the north; I will ascend above the heights of the clouds, I will be like the Most High'" (Isaiah 14:12-14).

Through lies and deception, Satan convinced one third of the heavenly angels to follow him in this rebellion. Finally, Satan and his angels were expelled from heaven.

This war that began in heaven has now come down to this earth.

"...Woe to the inhabitants of the earth and the sea! For the devil has come down to you, having great wrath, because he knows that he has a short time" (Revelation 12:12).

Satan has always pursued God's faithful people. And in these final centuries of earth's history, he now intensifies his attack against the church.

"Now when the dragon saw that he had been cast to the earth, he persecuted the woman who gave birth to the male Child. But the woman was given two wings of a great eagle, that she might fly into the wilderness to her place, where she is nourished for a time and times and half a time, from the presence of the serpent" (Revelation 12:13-14).

God, through the remnant, protected His truths throughout the Dark Ages; like through the Waldenses of Europe who remained faithful to God's commandments, including the seventh-day Sabbath of the fourth commandment. Yet, Satan was not through. As we have studied in the 5th and 6th trumpets, he now accelerates his war against God's faithful and the Holy Scriptures.

"And the dragon was enraged with the woman, and he went to make war with the rest of her offspring, who keep the commandments of God and have the testimony of Jesus Christ" (Revelation 12:17).

Satan's final attack against the last of the faithful remnant is here unleashed. Despite this, there are those through patient endurance in earth's final hours who remain faithful and keep God's commandments. God has not, however, left them alone to fight against Satan's deceptions. This group is identified here as having the testimony of Jesus Christ. This testimony is defined in Revelation as the 'spirit of prophecy'.

"...For the testimony of Jesus is the spirit of prophecy" (Revelation 19:10)

Earth's final faithful church will have an added blessing from God, needed for this time, the spiritual gift of prophecy. This prophetic gift is given to help guide them through the final attacks of Satan.

Revelation Chapter 13

Again in symbolic language, chapter 13 recaps the rise of Papal Rome as a persecuting power against God's faithful. This prophecy will repeat and expand the themes of the seals and trumpets as well as the prophecies of Daniel.

John, in a vision, sees a beast rising up out of the sea. With seven heads and ten horns, he had, "on his horns ten crowns and on his heads a blasphemous name". This beast was like a leopard with feet of a bear and a mouth of a lion. It was the dragon, Satan, who gave this beast his power and authority. This beast spoke blasphemies and was given authority for 42 months.

"Then he opened his mouth in blasphemy against God, to blaspheme His name, His tabernacle, and those who dwell in heaven" (Revelation 13:6).

This beast made war against the saints and overcame them:

"And all who dwell on the earth will worship him, whose names have not been written in the Book of Life of the Lamb slain from the foundation of the world" (Revelation 13:8).

This vision is a summary of the one found in chapter seven of Daniel. Like the four beasts came up out of the sea, this one does too. As an amalgamation of those described in chapter seven, this sea beast of Revelation also has a total of seven heads and ten horns. This beast represents the kingdom of Papal Rome, the apostate church-state union. Although in name it may be Christian, roots of pagan influence from the nations of the world have corrupted its doctrines. Satan is the author of this apostate church-state union. Through it he hoped to extinguish God's truth and the faithful remnant church. He also, through this great deception, wished to receive worship to himself.

Within verse three of chapter 13, we find a new detail concerning this beast power.

As we know, at the hands of France, Papal Rome received an apparently fatal wound, the apostate church seemed to be at her end. But, according to verse three, this wound would be healed and the entire world would wonder after the beast.

"I saw one of his heads as if it had been mortally wounded, and his deadly wound was healed. And all the world marveled and followed the beast. So they worshiped the dragon who gave authority to the beast; and they worshiped the beast, saying, 'Who is like the beast? Who is able to make war with him?'" (Revelation 13:3-4).

Here is a startling prediction. The apostate church-state union of the Roman Catholic Church would rise again. Like a phoenix from the flames, it would come back to life. The next section of chapter 13 will add further details to this fascinating prophecy.

In this section, another beast or nation is introduced beginning in verse 11. This beast, in contrast to the first beast, which arose from the symbolic sea of humanity, comes up out of the earth (in a relatively desolate place). This nation has as its horns or strengths of power, Christian characteristics of Christ the lamb, it is a Christian nation.

At the time when the Papal Church is coming to the end of its 1260-year rule, around the end of the 1700's, another nation comes upon the scene. This Christian nation arises from a place that unlike the populated nations of the old world, is relatively desolate. This nation, according to verse 12, becomes a world superpower that can cause the whole world to follow its dictates.

This nation can only be the United States of America. Coming to life as a sovereign nation, its birth in the late 1700's occurred at the time when the Papal Roman power was coming to an end in Europe. Formed as a Christian republic with freedom of religion, in the last two hundred years, it has risen to be an unparallel superpower, a nation of destiny.

Unfortunately, this nation would end up 'speaking like a dragon'. At a time when Papal Rome has recovered from its 'fatal' wound, the United States with its own church-state union of authority, will join with it to force the whole world to worship with this combined apostate power.

Roger Miller, M.D.

"And he exercises all the authority of the first beast in his presence, and causes the earth and those who dwell in it to worship the first beast, whose deadly wound was healed" (Revelation 13:12).

"He performs great signs, so that he even makes fire come down from heaven on the earth in the sight of men. And he deceives those who dwell on the earth by those signs which he was granted to do in the sight of the beast, telling those who dwell on the earth to make an image to the beast who was wounded by the sword and lived" (Revelation 13:13-14).

Through the influence of disguised and deceptive demonic supernatural manifestations, the apostate church-state union of authority within the United States uses its strength and political power to create a world religion. This is similar to, and in the image of the church-state Papal rule of the Dark Ages, it begins to speak or legislate like a 'dragon'. Most of the people are deceived to believe that this new religious order is the only hope for planet earth. People are told that this will bring an end to conflict between the different religions of the world. They believe it to be their only hope for peace and safety.

With all churches in union under the authority of the Roman church, and with the civil power and authority of the United States, a one-world religion is established. By its lethal military might, the United States gives breath and life to this one-world apostate religion. Through its influence, people are forced to worship as it dictates, even if it violates their conscience and beliefs. For fear of economic embargos or death, people are coerced to follow after the image to the Papal beast and receive its mark of authority.

"He was granted power to give breath to the image of the beast, that the image of the beast should both speak and cause as many as would not worship the image of the beast to be killed. And he causes all, both small and great, rich and poor,

free and slave, to receive a mark on their right hand or on their foreheads, and that no one may buy or sell except one who has the mark or the name of the beast, or the number of his name" (Revelation 13:15-17).

The mark or seal of authority of this apostate counterfeit system is what identifies those who support it. This mark, in contrast to the seal or mark of the 144 thousand, signifies the authority of Satan rather than God in their lives. As we have already seen in previous chapters, the forehead represents the mind and heart. The right hand symbolizes one's actions or behavior. The seal of God is His commandments written within the minds and hearts of His people, which will be manifested in the 'works' of their hands. In contrast, the mark of the beast is false commandments written in the mind or carried out in one's life. As a blasphemous power, Papal Rome tried to exercise its authority above that of God's by changing His commandments and God's set times. If you will remember from Daniel chapter seven, it says:

" He shall speak pompous [blasphemous] words against the Most High, shall persecute the saints of the Most High, and shall intend to change times and law . . ." (Daniel 7:25).

The fourth commandment, which identifies the God of the commandments as the creator of the heavens and the earth, was 'changed' by papal powers as a seal of their own authority. Of course, Satan was behind this attempt to usurp God's authority. The apostate church changed the Sabbath from the seventh-day that God had blessed and made holy, to the first day of the week, Sunday. This was in part as a memorial to the resurrection of Jesus on the first day of the week, Easter Sunday, as well as a compromise with pagan religions that worshiped the sun god on the venerable day of the sun. The problem is, there is no authority from the Bible to make such a change. In fact, it is this fourth commandment that is the very signature of God upon the Ten Commandments, the commandment that tells us who we are to worship. It is the Sabbath, as a memorial to creation and to the authority of our creator, that we are commanded to remember. This was given to mankind even before sin entered our planet. As we have already seen, it is this commandment that is the sign that we worship the true God of creation and that He alone can make and keep us holy.

It is this change of worship from the seventh-day Sabbath, commanded by the fourth commandment, to the first day of the week, that is the mark of authority of the beast and the image of the beast in Revelation chapter 13. All those who are deceived in their minds or follow because of fear, will receive the mark of this false beast authority(and of Satan who is behind this great deception).

"Here is wisdom. Let him who has understanding calculate the number of the beast, for it is the number of a man; His number is 666" (Revelation 13:18).

As a further identifying trait of the sea beast, the number of his name is given. Although not in practice today, numbering one's name or title with Roman numerals was common in the first century. This system gives a number value to letters within one's name. The official title of the Pope in Latin- their official language- written upon the coronation crown is VICARIVS FILII DEI-Vicar of the Son of God. With V=to 5, I=to1, L=to 50, C=to 100 and D=to 500 the total value is 666, a number of great importance to ancient Babylonian pagan worship. This number was worn as an amulet by priests of these pagan religions.

These prophecies, obviously, have not all been fulfilled at the time of this writing. It should be noted however, that Papal Rome has largely recovered from its fatal wound. Shortly after its demise in the late 1700's, a new pope was set up and by 1929 the apostate church had been given back all their church-state sovereignty and properties. In the last few decades, beginning during President Regan's administration, the United States has sent ambassadors to the Vatican and received their ambassadors. Pope

John Paul II in the last few years has brought the churches popularity to new record heights of recent history. It remains to be seen what will happen under the new Pope's rule. In addition, within the United States, there has been a great movement to gain political control by the protestant churches-to unite church and state, as well as a restoration of relationships between Protestants and Catholics by down playing their doctrinal differences. You can be sure these prophecies that have been understood and taught for nearly 200 years will come to pass!

Revelation Chapter 14

In chapter 14, God gives His final efforts to reach mankind and to warn them of the universal false system of worship. This chapter repeats and expands the prophecies of chapters 7, 10 and 11 of Revelation. In contrast to those with the mark and seal of the beast, these are the people that have the mark and seal of the true God of creation. As we have already seen, this symbolic 144 thousand are God's faithful. They will not receive the mark of the beast because their loyalty is to God and His commandments. These are the faithful who will be redeemed from the earth at Jesus' return. Like faithful 'virgins,' they have not partaken of the false system of worship, the false church. They follow only the Lamb and stand with Jesus and His kingdom. The final proclamation of truth is brought to the world by this faithful remnant and is proclaimed with a 'loud voice' to bring light to an otherwise dark place. These messages known as the 'Three Angels Messages,' are announced in Revelation 14:6-13.

"Then I saw another angel flying in the midst of heaven, having the everlasting gospel to preach to those who dwell on the earth-to every nation, tribe, tongue, and people-saying with a loud voice, 'Fear God and give glory to Him, for the hour of

His judgment has come; and worship Him who made heaven and earth, the sea and springs of water'" (Revelation 14:6-7).

This first angel's message, which is a universal message for all people, is to fear God and not the apostate church; to give glory to the true God not the false papal authority. It announces that the hour of God's judgment has come (since 1844 investigative judgment has begun in the heavenly sanctuary). It continues with a call to worship the true God of creation, the God identified in the fourth commandment. This message is a call back to true worship and faithfulness.

"And another angel followed, saying 'Babylon is fallen, is fallen, that great city, because she has made all nations drink of the wine of the wrath of her fornication'" (Revelation 14:8).

The clue to this message comes from the fifth chapter of Daniel. In this chapter, Belshazzar king of Babylon held a feast with all the nation's lords and rulers. In a state of drunkenness, he brought out the sacred vessels that had been stolen from the temple in Jerusalem, and used them in a worship service to the false gods of Babylon. As a 'last straw' the 'handwriting was on the wall' for Babylon and it fell that night to the armies of the Media-Persian Empire.

This story is used symbolically in Revelation chapter 14 to declare that the false church, symbolic Babylon, has fallen and is coming to its end. Like the ancient kingdom of Babylon fell because of its pagan apostasy and unholy religious alliance, it too would fall. Babylon, from is roots to the tower of Babel, means '*confusion*'. The false apostate church of Papal Rome as well as all those who hold doctrine not found in the Bible belong to symbolic Babylon, a confusion of good and evil ideas and teachings.

"Then a third angel followed them, saying with a loud voice, "If anyone worships the beast and his image, and receives his mark on his forehead or on his hand, he himself shall also drink of the wine of the wrath of God, which is poured out

full strength into the cup of His indignation. And he shall be tormented with fire and brimstone in the presence of the holy angels and in the presence of the Lamb. And the smoke of their torment ascends forever and ever; and they have no rest day or night, who worship the beast and his image, and who- ever receives the mark of his name" (Revelation 14:9-11).

The cry of the third angel is to get out of Babylon before you too must drink of the cup of God's wrath against her. We will see this wrath being poured out beginning in chapter 16 with the seven last plagues. The complete fall of spiritual Babylon and finally the second coming of Jesus will follow this. Ultimately, the final complete destruction of all evil in the lake of fire will occur at the white throne judgment at the conclusion of the mil- lennium. We will discuss all this in later chapters.

In contrast to the words of warning to those in Babylon, are these words of peace for the faithful.

"Here is the patience of the saints; here are those who keep the commandments of God and the faith of Jesus" (Revelation 14:12).

And a special message for those who are martyred or laid to rest before Jesus comes again:

"Blessed are the dead who die in the Lord from now on...that they may rest from their labors, and their works follow them" (Revelation 14:13).

Next, as the Great Controversy unfolds, is the scene of the second coming of Jesus and the harvest of the righteous as well as the final destruction of the wicked.

"And I looked, and behold, a white cloud, and on the cloud sat One like the Son of Man, having on His head a golden crown, and in His hand a sharp sickle. And another angel came out of the temple, crying with a loud voice to Him who sat on the cloud, "Thrust in Your sickle and reap, for the time

has come for You to reap, for the harvest of the earth is ripe. So He who sat on the cloud thrust in His sickle on the earth, and the earth was reaped." Then another angel came out of the temple, which is in heaven, he also having a sharp sickle. And another angel came out from the altar, who had power over fire, and he cried with a loud cry to him who had the sharp sickle, saying, "Thrust in your sharp sickle and gather the clusters of the vine of the earth, for her grapes are fully ripe." So the angel thrust his sickle into the earth and gathered the vine of the earth, and threw it into the great winepress of the wrath of God. And the winepress was trampled outside the city, and blood came out of the winepress, up to the horses' bridles, for one thousand six hundred furlongs" (Revelation 14:14-20).

In again metaphoric language, the final outcome of the saved and the lost is described as a harvest. Jesus used this metaphor.

"Let both grow together until the harvest, and at the time of harvest I will say to the reapers, "First gather together the tares and bind them in bundles to burn them, but gather the wheat into my barn" (Matthew 13:30).

At the conclusion of the cleansing of the heavenly sanctuary, Jesus will return and harvest his saints from the earth: both those who have died as well as all the righteous who remain alive. Even though the unsaved are killed at His coming, the final and complete destruction of the wicked, as we will see in chapter 20 of Revelation, occurs following the second resurrection at the end of the 1000 years. Like ripened grapes, the sins of the wicked and unrepentant are ready for harvest. God's cup of wrath has been filled and with salvation complete it is time for the final executive judgment against sin in the lake of fire. But before this, the seven last plagues and the fall of symbolic spiritual Babylon must occur.

Chapter 6

The Seven Last Plagues and the Fall of Babylon

Revelation Chapter 15 through Chapter 19:5

Revelation Chapter 15

"Then I saw another sign in heaven, great and marvelous; seven angels having the seven last plagues, for in them the wrath of God is complete" (Revelation 15:1).

Finally, the time has come for God Himself to pour out judgments upon all those who worship the beast and his image. These are 'strange acts' for a God who is longsuffering, merciful and not willing that any should perish but that all should come to repentance (2 Peter 3:9). But, like with Egypt of old, God is about to move in judgment plagues against the persecutors of His people and the unrepentant. Of the ten plagues that fell upon ancient Egypt, the last seven plagues did not fall upon the land of Goshen where the children of Israel were living. In similar fashion, Revelation's seven last plagues only fall upon the lost. Even though this will be a time of tribulation even for the elect, they will be protected from the effects of the plagues. Speaking of this time, the book of Mark says this:

"For in those days there will be tribulation, such as has not been from the beginning of creation which God created until this time, nor ever shall be. And unless the Lord had shortened those days, no flesh would be saved; but for the elect's sake, whom He chose, He shortened the days" (Mark 13:19, 20).

And from Psalms:

"A thousand may fall at your side, and ten thousand at your right hand; but it shall not come near you. Only with your eyes

shall you look, and see the reward of the wicked. Because you have made the Lord, who is my refuge, even the Most High, your habitation, no evil shall befall you, nor shall any plague come near your dwelling; for He shall give His angels charge over you, to keep you in all your ways" (Psalm 91:7-11).

Before the plagues are described, the future of those who have gained victory over the beast is unveiled again through the symbolic visual portal of the laver. Again, like the Israelites before their exodus from Egypt, they receive the assurance of deliverance and of God's protection from what is about to come upon the earth. Their final reward is portrayed along with their victory song at the completion of God's judgments upon the wicked.

"And I saw something like a sea of glass mingled with fire, and those who have the victory over the beast, over his image and over his mark and over the number of his name, standing on the sea of glass having harps of God. And they sing the song of Moses, the servant of God, and the song of the Lamb, saying: "Great and marvelous are Your works, Lord God Almighty! Just and true are Your ways, O King of the saints! Who shall not fear You, O Lord, and glorify your name? For you alone are holy. For all nations shall come and worship before You, for Your judgments have been manifested" (Revelation 15:2-4).

The final events of the heavenly sanctuary are about to unfold. The investigative judgment is now complete. All destinies are sealed. The reward of the wicked is about to be poured out followed by the reward of the righteous at Christ's return. Those who are holy will remain holy and those who are evil will remain evil.

"He who is unjust, let him be unjust still; he who is filthy, let him be filthy still; he who is righteous, let him be righteous still; he who is holy, let him be holy still" (Revelation 22:11).

"After these things I looked, and behold, the temple of the tabernacle of the testimony in heaven was opened. And out of

the temple came the seven angels having the seven plagues, clothed in pure bright linen, and having their chests girded with golden bands. Then one of the four living creatures gave to the seven angels seven golden bowls full of the wrath of God who lives forever and ever. The temple was filled with smoke from the glory of God and from His power, and no one was able to enter the temple till the seven plagues of the seven angels were completed" (Revelation 15:5-8).

Revelation Chapter 16

"Then I heard a loud voice from the temple saying to the seven angels, 'Go and pour out the bowls of the wrath of God on the earth'" (Revelation 16:1).

Men have put their faith in a false system of worship. Although Christian by name, it is consumed with counterfeit commandments, false gods and pagan beliefs. Like the plagues against the false gods of ancient Egypt, Revelation's plagues now fall on modern man's gods. Through the plagues, these are seen in truth to be nothing more than devices of destruction. God's mercy had provided a way of escape from the path of sin and death, but for all those who have turned away from this mercy, they must now reap the wind of their own destruction. Even though God is a God of great mercy, He is also a God of great justice. Those who refuse His mercy have now only to drink the cup of God's judgments against sin.

"So the first [angel] went and poured out his bowl upon the earth, and a foul and loathsome sore came upon the men who had the mark of the beast and those who worshiped his image" (Revelation 16:2).

This plague is described with both literal and symbolic language. The pouring out of the judgment from a bowl as well as the symbolism of the mark of the beast and the image of the beast are figurative, however, the effect of the plague as a loathsome sore is literal. Those who have trusted in the false god of themselves and their own works now see their true condition, full of disease. Leprosy sores were referred to symbolically in Old Testament times as an outward sign of ones inward condition of a diseased and sinful heart.

"Then the second angel poured out his bowl on the sea, and it become blood as of a dead man; and every living creature in the sea died" (Revelation 16:3).

Men have put their hopes in earthly kingdoms that have come up from the sea of humanity, and now these are seen for their true value, death. Like the plague of ancient Egypt, the sea is turned to blood.

"Then the third angel poured out his bowl on the rivers and springs of water, and they became blood" (Revelation 16:4).

The false, polluted doctrines of Papal Rome have caused great anguish and persecution to come upon the faithful. Now, God gives them blood to drink. Like false doctrines bring spiritual death, so also the impure water brings physical death.

"For they have shed the blood of saints and prophets, and You have given them blood to drink. For it is their just due" (Revelation 16:6).

"Then the fourth angel poured out his bowl on the sun, and power was given to him to scorch men with fire" (Revelation 16:8).

Men have refused to worship the true God of creation, the God of the Sabbath; and instead, have worshiped the creation itself. Paul in Romans says this:

"...who exchanged the truth of God for the lie, and worshiped and served the creature rather than the Creator..." (Romans 1:25). The sun, here representing the object of most pagan and false worship including the false Sabbath, turns into a power of pain and destruction.

"And men were scorched with great heat, and they blasphemed the name of God who has power over these plagues; and they did not repent and give Him glory" (Revelation 16:9).

Despite these plagues, like pharaoh in Egypt of old, they hardened their hearts against the true God who has power over all creation. Because they have severed their conscious from the influence of the Holy Spirit, there is no hope for them to see truth. The hour of their probation has closed and their fate is sealed. The earth is dying and despair is their lot.

"Then the fifth angel poured out his bowl on the throne of the beast, and his kingdom became full of darkness" (Revelation 16:10).

Having rejected the light of the 'three angels' messages, darkness now falls upon the center of apostate worship. The false 'light' and so-called 'enlightenment' of man is now seen as it truly is, darkness. Satan and his angels have appeared in supernatural manifestations to support the false system of worship. Now, these false gods and their darkness are revealed. This illusion of Satan, to appear as an angel of light, was foretold in 2 Corinthians.

"For such are false apostles, deceitful workers, transforming themselves into apostles of Christ. And no wonder! For Satan himself transforms himself into an angel of light. Therefore it is no great thing if his ministers also transform themselves into ministers of righteousness, whose end will be according to their works" (2 Corinthians 11;13-15).

"Then the sixth angel poured out his bowl on the great river Euphrates, and its water was dried up, so that the way of the kings from the east might be prepared" (Revelation 16:12).

The clue to this symbolic bowl Judgment is found in the story of the fall of ancient Babylon. Cyrus, the king of the Persian Empire, was prophetically called by name in Isaiah 44:28 over one hundred years before his birth. Cyrus was a type of shepherd and symbolic messiah, which God sent to conquer Babylon and to free His captive people. By diverting the river Euphrates that ran under the walls of Babylon, Cyrus was able to march his troops into the city and conquer it. It was Cyrus that would make the first decree for the Israelites to return to their home, Jerusalem, in the Promised Land.

As a part of the sixth bowl judgment, this story is used to symbolize the inevitable loss of support for symbolic spiritual Babylon. Because of the plagues, the support of the people dries up. This prepares the way for the true messiah from the east, Jesus, to come and take his people home–back to the heavenly promised land. Men have put their trust in this apostate church and now it too is seen to be false.

The support of the people is, in large part, due to the signs and miracles performed by Satan and his demons through their false prophets and the false christ. Jesus warned of this in Matthew. Talking about the end of time, He says this:

"For false christs and false prophets will arise and show great signs and wonders, so as to deceive, if possible, even the elect" (Matthew 24:24).

And from Revelation:

"And I saw three unclean spirits like frogs coming out of the mouth of the dragon, out of the mouth of the beast, and out of the mouth of the false prophet. For they are spirits of demons, performing signs [miracles KJV], which go out to the kings of the earth and of the whole world, to gather them to the battle of that great day of God Almighty...And they gathered them together to the place called in Hebrew, Armageddon" (Revelation 16:13-16).

"...for by your sorcery all the nations were deceived" (Revelation 18:23).

Again, this deceptive attack of Satan is described in Revelation chapter 19.

"Then the beast was captured, and with him the false prophet who worked signs [miracles KJV] in his presence, by which he deceived those who received the mark of the beast and those who worshiped his image" (Revelation 19:20).

And, as we have seen before from chapter 13 of Revelation:

"He performs great signs [wonders KJV] so that he even makes fire come down from heaven on the earth in the sight of men. And he deceives those who dwell on the earth by those signs [miracles KJV]…" (Revelation 13:13, 14).

Through these deceptions, Satan has gathered his people together against God and His faithful in the last and greatest spiritual battle on earth, the battle of Armageddon.

The word Armageddon is actually the combination of two Hebrew words: '*Har*', meaning *mountain*, and '*Megiddon*' (the Hebrew of '*Megiddo*') which is a plain and valley north of Jerusalem. In Zechariah this plain, where many battles were fought against the enemies of Israel, is mentioned as a place of great mourning.

"In that day there shall be a great mourning in Jerusalem, like the mourning at Hadad Rimmon in the plain of Megiddo [Megiddon in Hebrew]" (Zechariah 12:11).

Here in Revelation 16:16, it is the mountain of the plain of Megiddon that is the site for this great show down between the forces of evil and the faithful of God.

To understand this symbolism, we must again use an Old Testament story as our clue to unlock this mystery.

The story is of Elijah found in the book of 1 Kings chapter 18. In this story, under the control of the unholy church-state union of Ahab and Jezebel, Israel had fallen into deep apostasy and the worship of false gods. Because of this evil, God had sent a drought upon the land for three and one-half years. At the end of this period, Elijah presented Ahab with a challenge between himself, the servant of the true God, and the prophets of the false god Baal. This show-down was to occur at the top of Mount Carmel. This was a great mountain to the north that overlooked the plain of Megiddo. It was called in Hebrew, the mountain of Megiddon (Har megiddon or 'Armageddon'). In this demonstration of the power of the true God, God sent fire from heaven to consume the sacrifice upon the altar of Elijah. The prayers of the prophets of Baal went unanswered, and no fire fell upon their altar. God had limited Satan's power and did not allow him to deceive the people at that time.

In Revelation's last spiritual battle between good and evil, with Satan's power unrestricted, he has deceived the people. With signs and miracles, Satan has symbolically brought fire down from heaven upon the 'altar of Baal'. This is, to the deceived, proof that God is with them. This false Christianity, however, could not be further from God and His truth. Notice what Jesus says.

"Not everyone who says to Me, 'Lord, Lord,' shall enter the kingdom of heaven, but he who does the will of My Father in heaven. Many will say to Me in that day, 'Lord, Lord, have we not prophesied in Your name, cast out demons in Your name, and done many wonders in Your name?' And then I will declare to them, 'I never knew you; depart from Me, you who practice lawlessness!'" (Matthew 7:21-23).

As you can see, knowing God's will and doing it is very important. We can only know His will through His word in Scripture and we can only do it by letting Him live in us through His Holy Spirit. In the book of John, Jesus states it simply like this:

"If you love Me, keep My commandments" (John 14:15).

"If anyone loves Me, he will keep My word; and My Father will love him, and We will come to him and make Our home with him" (John 14:23).

Within the sixth-bowl judgment are these words of warning to the faithful church:

"Behold, I am coming as a thief. Blessed is he who watches, and keeps his garments, least he walk naked and they see his shame" (Revelation 16:15).

With a hint of desperation, Jesus pleads with the elect. Knowing the magnitude and potential of Satan's deceptions, their only hope is to be awake, watchful, and completely enveloped in righteousness and the word of God. This is a call today, to all who are in the same spiritual condition as those of the church in Laodicea. A call to repent and let God into your heart and buy from Him white robes of His righteousness.

"Then the seventh angel poured out his bowl into the air, and a loud voice came out of the temple of heaven, from the throne, saying, 'It is done!'" (Revelation 16:17).

This is one of four times in scripture that God makes the proclamation "It is done."

The first time was at the end of creation week, when on the Sabbath He rested from His work as creator.

"Thus the heavens and the earth, and all the host of them, were finished. And on the seventh day God ended His work which He had done, and He rested on the seventh day form all His work which He had done" (Genesis 2:1-2).

As His work of creation came to an end, Christ proclaimed through the Sabbath, that He was done with all the wonderful works of His creation. The second time was on the cross at the end of His work as Redeemer.

"...He [Jesus] said, "It is finished!" And bowing His head, He gave up His spirit" (John 19:30).

As Christ and our Redeemer, Jesus finished His work as the Lamb of God.

The third, "It is done", is heard now at the beginning of the seventh plague. Jesus states that with this plague His judgments will be completed. With His ministry as our High Priest, finished and the heavenly Day of Atonement complete, Jesus is about to don His kingly garments and come and rescue the faithful from the earth.

The fourth, as we will study in detail later, will be at the end of the 1000 years, the millennium. After the complete eradication of sin and the creation of the new heavens and the new earth, Jesus will proclaim, "It is done!"

"And there were noises and thunderings and lightnings; and there was a great earthquake, such a mighty and great earthquake as had not occurred since men were on the earth. Now the great city was divided in three parts, and the cities of the nations fell. And great Babylon was remembered before God, to give her the cup of the wine of the fierceness of His wrath. Then every island fled away, and the mountains were not found. And great hail from heaven fell upon men, every hailstone about the weight of a talent. And men blasphemed God because of the plague of the hail, since that plague was exceedingly great" (Revelation 16:18-21).

The condition of the unrepentant heart is proven by these seven last plagues. There is nothing God could have done that He had not already done that could reach a heart of sin that refused to yield to His creative power and be made new. God, through Isaiah with future prophetic insight, says this:

"What more could have been done to My vineyard that I have not done in it? Why then, when I expected it to bring forth good grapes, did it bring forth wild grapes? And now, please let Me tell you what I will do to My vineyard: I will take away its hedge, and it shall be burned..." (Isaiah 5:4 ,5).

Before the second coming of Christ is described in chapter 19, John reveals the final details of the fall of Babylon, the fall of the false systems of worship.

Revelation Chapter 17

"Then one of the seven angels who had the seven bowls came and talked with me, saying to me, "Come, I will show you the judgment of the great harlot who sits on many waters, with whom the kings of the earth committed fornication, and the inhabitants of the earth were made drunk with the wine of her fornication" (Revelation 17:1, 2).

In vision, John sees a symbolic woman sitting on a scarlet colored beast with seven heads and ten horns. The beast was full of blasphemy. The woman on the beast, is arrayed in purple and scarlet, and adorned with gold, precious stones and pearls. She is holding a golden cup full of abominations and the filthiness of her fornication. And on her forehead was written this:

"MYSTERY, BABYLON THE GREAT, THE MOTHER OF HARLOTS AND OF THE ABOMINATIONS OF THE EARTH" (Revelation 17:5).

The woman was drunk with the blood of the saints and martyrs of Jesus. John was very impressed with this strange image. What could this mean? The Angel then gives John a riddle to help solve the mystery:

"The beast that you saw was, and is not, and will ascend out of the bottomless pit and go to perdition. And those who dwell on the earth will marvel, whose names are not written in the Book of Life from the foundation of the world, when they see the beast that was, and is not, and yet is" (Revelation 17:8).

The riddle is followed by a series of clues and definitions to the symbols within the vision.

"The seven heads are seven mountains on which the woman sits. There are also seven kings. Five have fallen, one is, and the other has not yet come. And when he comes, he must

continue a short time. And the beast that was, and is not, is himself also the eighth, and is of the seven, and is going to perdition. And the ten horns which you saw are ten kings who have received no kingdom as yet, but they receive authority for one hour as kings with the beast. These are of one mind, and they will give their power and authority to the beast. These will make war with the Lamb, and the Lamb will overcome them, for He is Lord of lords and King of kings, and those who are with Him are called, chosen, and faithful. And he said to me, 'The waters which you saw, where the harlot sits, are peoples, multitudes, nations, and tongues. And the ten horns which you saw on the beast, these will hate the harlot, make her desolate and naked, eat her flesh and burn her with fire. For God has put it into their hearts to fulfill His purpose, to be of one mind, and to give their kingdom to the beast, until the words of God are fulfilled. And the woman whom you saw is that great city which reigns over the kings of the earth'" (Revelation 17:9-18).

Let's see if we can put this all together.

We have already seen many of these symbols used in Revelation. Remember our key to prophetic interpretation concerning the idea of repeating a prophecy and expanding the details? This vision is not something new, just a different perspective with added information. Let's review what we know, and add the new points of interest.

A woman is symbolic of the church. In chapter 12 a pure woman clothed with the sun represented the true faithful church. Here in chapter 17, the woman is a harlot. She is clothed in the same colors as were used by the priest in the earthly sanctuary- only the color blue is missing (which was symbolic for obedience to the Law of God). Unlike the faithful pure church, this church is unfaithful to Christ and has played the harlot with forbidden symbolic lovers. This symbolism of unfaithfulness in marriage, representing apostasy in the church, is used throughout scripture in both the Old and

New Testaments. One reference is found in James.

"Adulterers and adulteresses! Do you not know that friendship with the world is enmity with God? Whoever therefore wants to be a friend of the world makes himself an enemy of God" (James 4:4).

The woman, or unfaithful apostate church, is sitting upon a beast. A beast in prophecy, as we have seen many times before, is symbolic for a kingdom. This beast of Revelation chapter 17 has seven heads like the sea beast from chapter 13. The angel tells us that the seven heads represent seven mountains, which are also symbolic for nations or kingdoms. These nations apparently represent all the kingdoms that have influenced the church to become unfaithful and fall into apostasy. At the time the vision is given to John in the first century, five of these kingdoms had fallen, one was currently in power and one was yet in the future. From Old Testament scripture and prophecy, the five nations that had contributed to the apostasy of God's covenant people of Israel were: Egypt, during Israel's 400-year captivity there; Assyria, who took captive the northern kingdom of Israel; Babylon, who took captive the southern kingdom of Judea; Media-Persia; and Greece. The kingdom that influenced the new covenant church and was in power in John's day was Rome, and the power that was yet to come was Papal Rome.

Therefore, the beast represents a combination of all previous pagan influence upon both the Old and New Testament churches that had contributed to its fall into apostasy. Notice that the amalgamated beast at the end time would be one of the original seven kingdoms that had been in power. It would loose its power but would come to life again to give support to the final apostate church-state power upon the earth, symbolic Babylon. It would be, "the beast that was, and is not, and yet is". We have already discovered this power to be the Papal Roman church that recovered from its deadly wound. In other words, the final apostate power would 'ride upon the back' of revived Papal

Rome. Again, this is nothing new. The final apostate power, when it was described as an image to the sea beast in chapter 13, also took its power and authority from the beast that was wounded by the sword and lived.

In addition, this beast power has ten horns that represent ten divisions of strength of the revived apostate church-state union. These ten kings or kingdoms of its civil strength are yet future to John's day but for a short time would have authority. They would give their authority to the beast for the purpose of spiritual warfare against the kingdom of Jesus- the lamb kingdom. The waters, that in vision supported the beast and its harlot rider, were symbolic of the support of the people of the earth that gave rise to these apostate powers.

Notice that, like we saw in the 6th plague, the support dries up and the ten kings turn upon the woman and burn her with fire. This has interesting symbolism when considering the outcome of a harlot in Old Testament times. Usually, when a harlot was found out, she would be stoned to death. Only if she were the daughter of a priest would she be burned (a fitting symbol for the unfaithful apostate church and church-state world religion). The title upon the forehead of the harlot woman is Babylon the Great. As we have seen, this symbolic spiritual Babylon represents the confusion between truth and error that would exist within the 'mind' or teachings of the apostate church. Also, she is labeled the mother of harlots. All those churches that pay homage to her false doctrines are also being unfaithful to Christ and represent symbolic daughter harlots.

Let's summarize.

The harlot woman is the final apostate church state-union upon earth, symbolic spiritual Babylon. She was described as an image to the sea beast of Papal Rome in chapter 13. She would rise in power upon the back of papal Rome with the support of this previously wounded, but now healed, apostate power. Papal

Rome, of course, was a combination of Christianity and pagan influences from the nations that had preceded it. This mother harlot would have daughters, also harlots, which represent the protestant churches that still give her honor by following her false teachings and doctrines. This final apostate image to Papal Rome would, for a short time, receive the support of the people and the ruling kingdoms or nations. But this support, partly because of the last plagues, would be withdrawn and her fate would be like the harlot daughter of a priest in Old Testament times. She would be burned with fire. She will come to her end. Babylon will fall.

Revelation Chapter 18

"After these things I saw another angel coming down from heaven, having great authority, and the earth was illuminated with his glory. And he cried mightily with a loud voice saying, "Babylon the great is fallen, is fallen, and has become a habitation of demons, a prison for every foul spirit, and a cage for every unclean and hated bird! For all the nations have drunk of the wine of the wrath of her fornication, the kings of the earth have committed fornication with her, and the merchants of the earth have become rich through the abundance of her luxury." And I heard another voice form heaven saying, "Come out of her, my people, lest you share in her sins, and lest you receive of her plagues. For her sins have reached to heaven, and God has remembered her iniquities. Render to her just as she rendered to you, and repay her double according to her works; in the cup which she has mixed, mix for her double. In the measure that she glorified herself and lived luxuriously, in the same measure give her torment and sorrow; for she says in her heart, 'I sit as queen, and am no widow, and will not see sorrow.' Therefore her plagues will come in one day-death and mourning and famine. And she will be utterly burned with fire, for strong is the Lord God who judges her" (Revelation 18: 1-8).

Here, we see the message of the three angels from chapter 14 reemphasized. Like Babylon of old, spiritual Babylon will fall. At a time when all seems spiritually dark, this message of light is given. This is the final message to the world given by the remnant faithful church of spiritual Israel in earth's last hours. This is a message to be faithful to God and to keep His truth. A call to come out of Babylon before it is to late and you share in her destruction. This message is for us today.

Are you being faithful to God and His commandments? Do you know Jesus and are you allowing Him to live out His goodness to others through you? Are the teachings and doctrines of your church from the Bible or from Papal Rome, tradition and paganism? Remember the words of Jesus quoting from Isaiah:

"These people draw near to Me with their mouth, and honor Me with their lips, but their heart is far from Me. And in vain they worship Me, teaching as doctrines the commandments of men'" *(Matthew 15:8-9).*

This is the time to hear His voice and join God's faithful remnant that keep the commandments of God and have the testimony of Jesus.

-A people who proclaim the literal, visible, soon second coming of Christ.

-A people who denounce the pagan teaching of life after death and uphold the Bible truth that death is a sleep-like state until the resurrection (the dead do not know anything and cannot communicate with the living).

-A people who have not forgotten the seventh-day Sabbath of the fourth commandment and by God's grace keep it holy.

-A people who reject the false Papal teaching of the eternal existence of sin and the eternal infliction of pain and suffering upon the lost, but rather uphold the Bible truth of an end to sin and a final eradication of Satan, sin, and unrepentant sinners in the lake of fire at the close of the millennium.

-A people who have the testimony of Jesus- the prophetic gift of prophecy.

-A people who understand the symbolism of the earthly sanctuary in relationship to the heavenly sanctuary and are proclaiming that the hour of judgment has come.

-A people who are worshiping the true God of creation not the false apostate church of Papal Rome or her daughters.

-And a people who are faithful to the Bible truths of the early apostolic church including: baptism by immersion; the non-literal symbolism of the ordinance of the communion; the priesthood of all believers to take their sins to Jesus for forgiveness, without an earthly priest or payment of money; and the truth that it is God alone through His grace and because of the sacrifice of Jesus who can create in us a clean heart and cleanse us from all unrighteousness.

Now, right now, is the time to decide to follow JESUS IN TRUTH!

"Today, if you will hear His voice: do not harden your hearts…" (Psalm 95:7, 8).

Revelation 18:9-24, recounts the fall of Babylon and the lament of those who appeared to prosper under her reign. The kings of the earth through their unholy union with the apostate church had felt themselves to be rich yet they were poor in true spiritual worth. This sad statement is made concerning the false church:

"And the fruit that your soul longed for has gone from you, and all the things which are rich and splendid have gone from you, and you shall find them no more at all" (Revelation 18:14).

Only by following God in truth can we find peace of heart and the fruit of His Holy Spirit. This fruit, in the end, is the only thing of real value.

"But the fruit of the Spirit is love, joy, peace, longsuffering, kindness, goodness, faithfulness, gentleness, self-control. Against such there is no law, and those who are Christ's have crucified the flesh with its passions and desires. If we live in the Spirit, let us also walk in the Spirit" (Galatians 5:22-23).

At Babylon's fall the nations of the earth symbolically weep and wail stating:

"Alas, alas that great city that was clothed in fine linen, purple, and scarlet, and adorned with gold and precious stones and pearls! For in one hour such great riches came to nothing" (Revelation 18:16, 17).

And these words, at last to vindicate the martyred souls of the fifth seal:

"Rejoice over her, O heaven, and you holy apostles and prophets, for God has avenged you on her!" (Revelation 18:20).

And this final symbolic act by a mighty angel:

"Then a mighty angel took up a stone like a great millstone and threw it into the sea, saying, 'Thus with violence the great city Babylon shall be thrown down, and shall not be found anymore... For your merchants were the great men of the earth, for by your sorcery all the nations were deceived. And in her was found the blood of prophets and saints, and of all who were slain on the earth'" (Revelation 18:21, 23, 24).

Like Rome was portrayed in the second trumpet as a symbolic mountain falling into the sea, and prophecies concerning ancient Babylon told of a mountain going down under the waves, here, spiritual Babylon suffers the same fate.

Revelation Chapter 19

"After these things I heard a loud voice of a great multitude in heaven, saying, "Alleluia! Salvation and glory and honor and power to the Lord our God! For true and righteous are His judgments, because He has judged the great harlot who corrupted the earth with her fornication; and He has avenged on her the blood of His servants shed by her." Again they said, 'Alleluia! And her smoke rises up forever and ever!'" **(Revelation 19:1-3).**

The false church has fallen and her destruction is complete and everlasting. With the fall of Babylon, it is time for Jesus to return.

Chapter 7

Controversy Ended and All Things Made New

Revelation Chapter 19:6 through Chapter 22

"And I heard, as it were, the voice of a great multitude, as the sound of many waters and as the sound of mighty thunderings, saying, "Alleluia! For the Lord God Omnipotent reigns! Let us be glad and rejoice and give Him glory, for the marriage of the Lamb has come, and His wife has made herself ready." And to her it was granted to be arrayed in fine linen, clean and bright, for the fine linen is the righteous acts of the saints" (Revelation 19:6-8).

One of man's most joyous occasions is used to symbolize the union of the faithful church with Christ at His second coming, the marriage. The faithful, through surrender to God, have been clothed in the light of His truth and character. They have yielded to His power of grace, to work in them to will and to do of His good pleasure. The true works of God have been manifested in their lives as they have served God and others in unselfish labor. They are adorned with a meek and gentle spirit ready to meet their 'betrothed husband,' Christ.

"Then I saw heaven opened, and behold, a white horse. And He who sat on him was called Faithful and True, and in righteousness He judges and makes war. His eyes were like a flame of fire, and on His head were many crowns. He had a name written that no one knew except Himself. He was clothed with a robe dipped in blood, and His name is called The Word of God. And the armies of heaven, clothed in fine linen, white and clean, followed Him on white horses. Now out of His mouth goes a sharp sword, that with it He should strike the nations. And He Himself will rule them with a rod of iron. He Himself treads the winepress of the fierceness and wrath of Almighty God. And He has on His robe and on His thigh a

**name written: KING OF KINGS AND LORD OF LORDS"
(Revelation 19:11-16).**

The most anticipated moment of Revelation has come. Jesus,
the word of God made flesh, has fulfilled His promise and
returned to earth. Riding a symbolic white horse of victory like
the first century church of the first seal in Revelation chapter six,
He returns. This time not as a Lamb to suffer, but rather as King
of kings and Lord of lords. With the joy of a bride on her wedding
day, the faithful are prepared to meet Him. With one voice they
proclaim:

*"Behold, this is our God; we have waited for Him, and He
will save us. This is the Lord; we have waited for Him; we will be
glad and rejoice in His salvation" (Isaiah 25:9).*

The 'rock' kingdom has come to strike the nations and deliver
it's people. Not just one ruler among many, but the ruler of all
nations and people, Christ comes crowned with many crowns.
What to the saved is great joy and happiness, to the lost is total
despair, and they exclaim to the mountains and rocks:

**"Fall on us and hide us from the face of Him who sits on the
throne and from the wrath of the Lamb!" (Revelation 6:16).**

With their false gods fallen, they now look upon those they
have persecuted, as radiant beams of light encircle them. To their
horror, those they have despised and hated are now revealed as
the true sons and daughters of God.

From the throne of Christ comes power and light so radiant,
that the earth quakes before it. And what to the saved is the resur-
recting and transforming power of eternal life, to the lawless
wicked is death and destruction.

*"...whom the Lord will consume with the breath of His mouth
and destroy with the brightness of His coming" (2 Thessalonians
2:8).*

"And the rest were killed with the sword which proceeded

from the mouth of Him who sat on the horse" (Revelation 19:21).

"For the indignation of the Lord is against all nations, and His fury against all their armies; He has utterly destroyed them, He has given them over to the slaughter. Also their slain shall be thrown out; their stench shall rise from their corpses, and the mountains shall be melted with their blood" (Isaiah 34:2, 3).

All the false systems of worship are destroyed in the presence of the true God. The beast with his false prophets all come to their end.

With the wicked destroyed and only the righteous remaining, the voice of Jesus is heard as He calls His sleeping saints from their graves. Paul describes these moments like this:

"For the Lord Himself will descend from heaven with a shout, with the voice of an archangel, and with the trumpet of God. And the dead in Christ will rise first. Then we who are alive and remain shall be caught up together with them in the clouds to meet the Lord in the air. And thus we shall always be with the Lord" (1 Thessalonians 4:16, 17).

What a victorious moment for the faithful church! When earth seems to be at its darkest hour, Christ comes with his armies of angels to redeem the faithful.

Revelation Chapter 20

Now, the redeemed of the earth return with Jesus and His angels to heaven to live and reign with Him for a thousand years.

"And I saw thrones, and they sat on them, and judgment was committed to them. And I saw the souls of those who had been beheaded for their witness to Jesus and for the word of God, who had not worshiped the beast or his image, and had not

received his mark on their foreheads or on their hands. And
they lived and reigned with Christ for a thousand years…This
is the first resurrection…Blessed and holy is he who has part
in the first resurrection. Over such the second death has no
power, but they shall be priests of God and of Christ, and
shall reign with Him a thousand years" (Revelation 20:4-6).**

The earth at this time is completely void of human life. The
bodies of the slain wicked lie scattered over the face of the earth
and the tombs of the lost remain closed and within the earth.
These will have part in the second resurrection and second death
of the wicked at the end of the 1000 years.

**"But the rest of the dead did not did not live again until the
thousand years were finished…" (Revelation 20:5).**

The first resurrection has past. The saints from all ages have
been resurrected and taken alive to live with Christ. As priests in
the temple of God, they now have part in the judgment of the
wicked and the fallen angels. All those who have rejected the sacrifice of Jesus, and did not have their sins recorded as forgiven
and finally cleansed from the heavenly sanctuary, must now bear
their own guilt in this final investigative judgment. Paul talks of
this judgment in 1 Corinthians 6:2-3.

"Do you not know that the saints will judge the world? And if
the world will be judged by you, are you unworthy to judge the
smallest matters? Do you not know that we shall judge angels?"

During this 1000-year judgment in heaven, with the earth
lying in waste and desolate; Satan by chains of circumstance is
bound, without anyone to tempt or deceive. He had desired to be
like God, now God gives him the earth in a lifeless condition similar to how it was prior to the Genesis creation. For a thousand
years in this prison he can contemplate what his rebellion and war
has cost. The path of Satan is despair, desolation and death.

**"Then I saw an angel coming down from heaven, having the
key to the bottomless pit and a great chain in his hand. He**

laid hold of the dragon, that serpent of old, who is the Devil and Satan, and bound him for a thousand years; and he cast him into the bottomless pit, and shut him up, and set a seal on him, so that he should deceive the nations no more till the thousand years were finished. But after these things he must be released for a little while" (Revelation 20:1-3).

Now Satan (and the lost) at the conclusion of the thousand year judgment, will meet their final fate.

"Now when the thousand years have expired, Satan will be released from his prison and will go out to deceive the nations which are in the four corners of the earth, Gog and Magog, to gather them together to battle, whose number is as the sand of the sea" (Revelation 20:7, 8).

Jesus and the saints in the New Jerusalem return to this earth at the conclusion of the 1000 years. God resurrects the dead who were slain at Jesus second coming and all those who did not have part in the first resurrection. This is the second resurrection, the resurrection of the wicked. Satan is then 'unbound' and with his followers, the deceived and unrepentant from all ages, surround the New Jerusalem with the intent of taking the city and killing all those inside, including Jesus. Like Gog and Magog, mortal enemies of ancient Israel of the Old Testament, they prepare to make war on the city.

"But outside [the city] are dogs and sorcerers and sexually immoral and murderers and idolaters, and whoever loves and practices a lie" (Revelation 22:15).

"They went up on the breadth of the earth and surrounded the camp of the saints and the beloved city" (Revelation 20: 9).

With all who have ever lived, now alive upon the earth, both the saints inside the city and the wicked outside of the city, the final sentence is pronounced upon the wicked.

Opened to everyone's eyes are the Book of Life and the books of record. Works of the saved from the Book of Life (the works of faith in Jesus), are a stark contrast to the now reveled secrets and unrepentant works of the lost. Jesus, as judge of all the earth, is seen sitting upon a great white throne where every eye can see.

"Then I saw a great white throne and Him who sat on it, from whose face the earth and the heaven fled away. And there was found no place for them. And I saw the dead, small and great, standing before God, and books were opened. And another book was opened, which is the Book of Life. And the dead were judged according to their works, by the things, which were written in the books. And the sea gave up the dead who were in it, and Death and Hades delivered up the dead who were in them. And they were judged, each on according to his works" (Revelation 20:11-13).

All of the lost, including Satan and his angels, for a moment, recognize the justness of God and bow the knee to Him. Paul quoting from Isaiah says this:

"As I live, says the Lord, Every knee shall bow to Me, and every tongue shall confess to God" (Romans 14:11).

And again in Philippians:

"Therefore God also has highly exalted Him and given Him the name which is above every name, that at the name of Jesus every knee should bow, of those in heaven, and of those on earth, and of those under the earth, and that every tongue should con-fess that Jesus Christ is Lord, to the glory of God the Father" (Philippians 2:9-11).

Following this moment of submission, again anger and hatred fill the hearts of the lost and they rush to take the city and pull Jesus from his throne and if allowed would crucify Him again. Despite all this evidence, their hearts are still determined to do evil. All created beings can see that there is no hope for the wicked and God's judgment is just. The final executive judgments now fall upon them.

"And fire came down from God out of heaven and devoured them. And the devil, who deceived them, was cast into the lake of fire and brimstone where the beast and the false prophet are. And they will be tormented day and night forever and ever…Then Death and Hades were cast into the lake of fire. This is the second death. And anyone not found written in the Book of Life was cast into the lake of fire" (Revelation 20:9, 10, 14, 15).

"But the cowardly, unbelieving, abominable, murderers, sexually immoral, sorcerers, idolaters, and all liars shall have their part in the lake which burns with fire and brimstone, which is the second death" (Revelation 21:8).

This final destruction and eradication of Satan and his angels, of all false gods and systems of worship, of sin and sinners, and even of death and the grave itself, is spoken of throughout Scripture as the final and eternal end to the sin rebellion.

"For behold, the day is coming, burning like an oven, and all the proud yes, all who do wickedly will be stubble. And the day which is coming shall burn them up," says the Lord of hosts, 'That will leave them neither root nor branch…You shall trample the wicked, for they shall be ashes under the soles of your feet on the day that I do this," Says the Lord of hosts" (Malachi 4:1, 3).

"For evildoers shall be cut off; but those who wait on the Lord they shall inherit the earth. For yet a little while and the wicked shall be no more; indeed, you will look carefully for his place, but it shall be no more. But the meek shall inherit the earth, and shall delight themselves in the abundance of peace…But the wicked shall perish; and the enemies of the Lord, like the splendor of the meadows, shall vanish. Into smoke they shall vanish away" (Psalm 37:9-11, 20).

"…when the Lord Jesus is revealed from heaven with His mighty angels, in flaming fire taking vengeance on those who do not know God, and on those who do not obey the gospel of our

Lord Jesus Christ. *These shall be punished with everlasting destruction from the presence of the Lord and from the glory of His power, when He comes, in that Day, to be glorified in His saints and to be admired among all those who believed"* *(2 Thessalonians 1:7-10).*

The effect of this hell, or final second death in the lake of fire, will be everlasting and eternal. Sin and wickedness will not arise again.

"He will make an utter end of it. Affliction will not rise up a second time...they shall be devoured like stubble fully dried" *(Nahum 1:9, 10).*

And speaking prophetically of Satan's future, Ezekiel writes this:

"Therefore I [God] brought fire from your midst; it devoured you, and I turned you to ashes upon the earth in the sight of all who saw you...You have become a horror, and shall be no more forever" *(Ezekiel 28:18, 19).*

Sin at last is gone! God is ready to fulfill all His promises made to the seven churches, and to those of all ages who have overcome.

Revelation Chapter 21

"Now I saw a new heaven and a new earth, for the first heaven and the first earth had passed away" (Revelation 21:1).

Jesus recreates a new home for the saved, a new earth. With the New Jerusalem as its capital city, the throne of God now resides upon the earth.

"Then I, John, saw the holy city, New Jerusalem, coming down out of heaven from God, prepared as a bride adorned

Roger Miller, M.D.

for her husband. And I heard a loud voice from heaven saying, 'Behold, the tabernacle of God is with men, and He will dwell with them, and they shall be His people, and God Himself will be with them and be their God. And God will wipe away every tear from their eyes; there shall be no more death, nor sorrow, nor crying; and there shall be no more pain, for the former things have passed away.' Then He who sat on the throne said, 'Behold, I make all things new.' And He said to me, 'Write, for these word are true and faithful.' And He said to me. 'It is done! I am the Alpha and the Omega, the Beginning and the End. I will give of the fountain of the water of life freely to him who thirsts. He who overcomes shall inherit all things, and I will be his God and he shall be My son'" (Revelation 21:2-7).

No more pain, no more sorrow, no more death, no more crying anymore! What on earth could be worth missing this? Things of this earth will not satisfy the need of your heart, but Jesus offers to quench the thirst of your soul with living water from the fountain of life.

Chapter 21, verse 9 through chapter 22, verse 4 describes the glory and the splendor of the New Jerusalem. Here are excerpts from these verses.

"And her light was like a most precious stone, like a jasper stone, clear as crystal. Also she had a great and high wall with twelve gates, and twelve angels at the gates, and names written on them, which are the names of the twelve tribes of the children of Israel: three gates on the east, three gates on the north, three gates on the south, and three gates on the west. Now the wall of the city had twelve foundations, and on them were the names of the twelve apostles of the Lamb…And the city is laid out as a square…Its length, breadth and height are equal (12,000 furlongs or 1380 miles)…its wall: one hundred and forty-four cubits…And the construction of its wall was of jasper; and the city was pure gold…And the foundations of the wall of the city were adorned with all kinds of precious stones…And the twelve gates were twelve pearls…And the street of the city was pure gold, like transparent glass…the Lord God Almighty and the Lamb are its temple…And the city had no need of the sun…for the glory of God illuminated it, and the Lamb is its light. And the nations of those who are saved shall walk in its light, and the kings of the earth bring their glory and honor into it. Its gates shall not be shut…

Revelation Chapter 22

And he showed me a pure river of water of life, clear as crystal, proceeding from the throne of God and of the Lamb. In the middle of its street, and on either side of the river, was the tree of life, which bore twelve fruits, each tree yielding its fruit every month. The leaves of the tree were for the healing of the nations. And there shall be no more curse, but the throne of God and of the Lamb shall be in it, and His servants shall serve Him. They shall see His face, and His name shall be on their foreheads. And there shall be no night there: They need no lamp nor light of the sun, for the Lord God gives them light. And they shall reign forever and ever."

John concludes the book of Revelation with Jesus' final appeal to the churches and to you and me.

"Behold, I am coming quickly! Blessed is he who keeps the words of the prophecy of this book" (Revelation 22:7).

"And behold, I am coming quickly, and My reward is with Me, to give to every one according to his work. I am the Alpha and the Omega the Beginning and the End, the First and Last" (Revelation 22:12-13).

"Blessed are those who do His commandments, that they may have the right to the tree of life, and may enter through the gates into the city" (Revelation 22:14).

"...Surely I am coming quickly" (Revelation 22:20)

"And the Spirit and the bride say, 'Come!' And let him who hears say, 'Come!' And let him who thirsts come. And whoever desires, let him take the water of life freely" (Revelation 22:17).

Will you come?!

"The grace of our Lord Jesus Christ be with you all. Amen" (Revelation 22:21).